EASY POP MELODIES

FOR HORN

ISBN 978-1-4803-8434-7

HAL•LEONARD®
CORPORATION

7777 W. Bluemound Rd. P.O. Box 13819 Milwaukee, WI 53213

Visit Hal Leonard Online at
www.halleonard.com

ALL MY LOVING

HORN

Words and Music by JOHN LENNON
and PAUL McCARTNEY

Fast
Dm G C
Close your eyes and I'll kiss you. To - mor - row I'll
tend that I'm kiss - ing the lips I am
Am F Dm
miss you. Re - mem - ber I'll al - ways be
miss - ing and hope that my dreams will come
B♭ G Dm G
true.
true.
And then while I'm a - way I'll write
C Am F
home ev - 'ry day, and I'll send all my
G C
1. 2.
lov - ing to you. I'll pre - All my
Am A♭+ C
lov - ing I will send to you. All my
Am A♭+ C
lov - ing, dar - ling, I'll be true.

BEAUTY AND THE BEAST

from Walt Disney's BEAUTY AND THE BEAST

HORN

Lyrics by HOWARD ASHMAN
Music by ALAN MENKEN

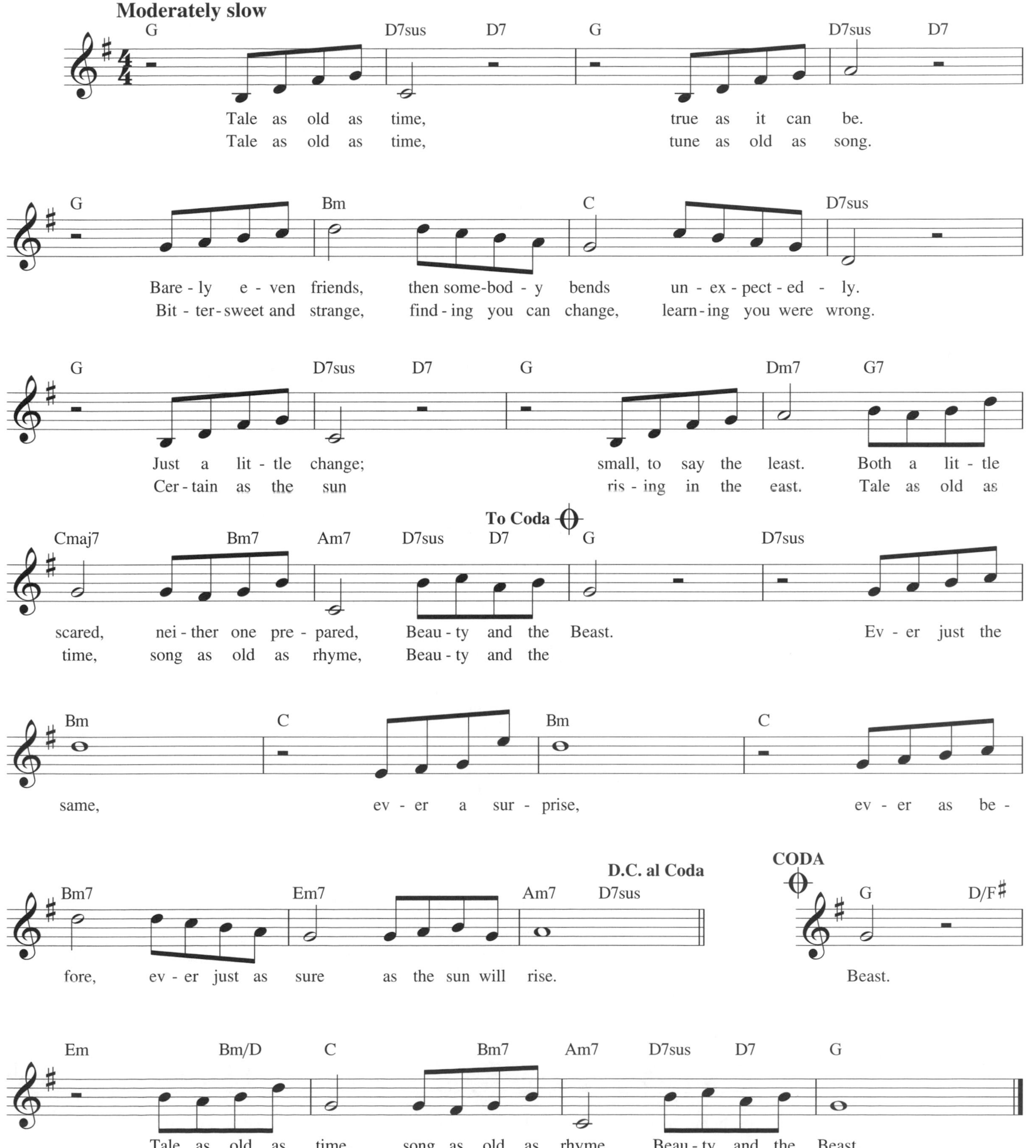
Moderately slow
G
D7sus
D7
G
D7sus
D7
Tale as old as time, true as it can be.
Tale as old as time, tune as old as song.
G
Bm
C
D7sus
Bare - ly e - ven friends, then some-bod - y bends un - ex - pect - ed - ly.
Bit - ter-sweet and strange, find - ing you can change, learn - ing you were wrong.
G
D7sus
D7
G
Dm7
G7
Just a lit - tle change; small, to say the least. Both a lit - tle
Cer - tain as the sun ris - ing in the east. Tale as old as
To Coda
Cmaj7
Bm7
Am7
D7sus
D7
G
D7sus
scared, nei - ther one pre - pared, Beau - ty and the Beast. Ev - er just the
time, song as old as rhyme, Beau - ty and the
Bm
C
Bm
C
same, ev - er a sur - prise, ev - er as be -
D.C. al Coda
CODA
Bm7
Em7
Am7
D7sus
G
D/F#
fore, ev - er just as sure as the sun will rise. Beast.
Em
Bm/D
C
Bm7
Am7
D7sus
D7
G
Tale as old as time, song as old as rhyme, Beau - ty and the Beast.

© 1991 Walt Disney Music Company and Wonderland Music Company, Inc.
All Rights Reserved Used by Permission

BLOWIN' IN THE WIND

HORN

Words and Music by
BOB DYLAN

Moderately
F Bb F
How man - y roads must a man walk down be -
How man - y years can a moun - tain ex - ist be -
Bb F
fore you call him a man?
fore it is washed to the sea?
Bb F
How man - y seas must a white dove sail be -
How man - y years can some peo - ple ex - ist be -
Bb C
fore she sleeps in the sand?
fore they're al - lowed to be free?
F Bb F
How man - y times must the can - non - balls fly be -
How man - y times can a man turn his head and pre -
Bb F
fore they're for - ev - er banned?
tend that he just does - n't see?
The
Bb C F Bb
an - swer, my friend, is blow - in' in the wind. The
C F
an - swer is blow - in' in the wind.

CAN YOU FEEL THE LOVE TONIGHT

from Walt Disney Pictures' THE LION KING

HORN

Music by ELTON JOHN
Lyrics by TIM RICE

Moderately
C G/B C G/B
There's a calm surrender to the rush of day
C G/B Am7 D
when the heat of a rolling wind can't be turned away.
C G/B C G/B
An enchanted moment, and it sees me through.
C Em F D
It's enough for this restless warrior just to be with you. And
G D/F♯ Em C
can you feel the love tonight?
can you feel the love tonight,
G C A/C♯ D C
It is where we are. It's enough
how it's laid to rest? It's enough
G/B Em Em/D C Am G/B 1. C A/C♯
for this wide-eyed wanderer that we got this far.
to make kings and vagabonds believe the
D 2. C D7sus C/G G
And very best.

CAN'T HELP FALLING IN LOVE

HORN

Words and Music by GEORGE DAVID WEISS,
HUGO PERETTI and LUIGI CREATORE

Moderately
F Am Dm B♭ F C7
Wise men say on - ly fools rush in, but
Shall I stay? Would it be a sin if
B♭ C7 F Gm F C7 F
I can't help fall - ing in love with you.
I can't help fall - ing in love with you?
Am E7 Am E7 Am E7
Like a riv - er flows sure - ly to the sea, dar - ling, so it goes,
Am D7 Gm C7 F Am
some things are meant to be. Take my
Dm B♭ F C7 B♭ C7
hand; take my whole life too, for I can't
F Gm F C7 F
help fall - ing in love with you, for
B♭ C7 F Gm F C7 F
I can't help fall - ing in love with you.

CLOCKS

Words and Music by GUY BERRYMAN,
JON BUCKLAND, WILL CHAMPION
and CHRIS MARTIN

HORN

Moderately
C
Gm
The lights go out and I can't be saved. Tides that I tried to
Con - fu - sion nev - er stops, clos - ing walls and
Dm
C
Gm
swim a - gainst have brought me down up - on my knees.
tick - ing clocks. Gonna come back and take you home. I
Dm
C
Oh, I beg, I beg and plead, sing - ing… Come out of
could not stop; that you know now, sing - ing… Come out up -
Gm
Dm
things un - said. Shoot an ap - ple off my head, and - a,
on my seas. Curse missed op - por - tu - ni - ties. Am I
C
Gm
trou - ble that can't be named. A ti - ger's wait - ing
a part of the cure, or am I part of
Dm
C
Gm
to be tamed, sing - ing…
the dis - ease, sing - ing…
You are.
Dm
C
Gm
Dm
C
You are.

DAYDREAM BELIEVER

HORN

Words and Music by
JOHN STEWART

Moderately
F
Gm
Oh, I could hide 'neath the wings of the
You once thought of me as a
Am
B♭
F
Dm
blue - bird as she sings. The six o - 'clock a - larm would nev - er
white knight on his steed. Now you know how hap - py I can
G
C
F
Gm
ring. But it rings and I rise, wipe the
be. Oh, and our good times start and end with - out
Am
B♭
F
Dm
sleep out of my eyes. My shav - ing ra - zor's
dol - lar one to spend. But how much, ba - by,
Gm
C
F
B♭
C
cold and it stings.
do we real - ly need?
Cheer up, sleep - y
Am
B♭
C
Dm
B♭
F
Jean. Oh, what can it mean to a day - dream be -
B♭
F
Dm
G
C
F
liev - er and a home - com-ing queen?

DON'T KNOW WHY

HORN

Words and Music by
JESSE HARRIS

Moderately
Cmaj7 C7 Fmaj7 E+ Am7 D7
I wait - ed till I saw the sun. Don't know why I
When I saw the break of day, wished that I could
Some - thing has to make you run. Don't know why I
G7sus C Cmaj7 C7 Fmaj7 E+
did - n't come. Left you by the house of fun.
fly a - way 'stead of kneel - ing in the sand,
did - n't come. Feel as emp - ty as a drum.
1.
Am7 D7 G7sus C Am7 D7
Don't know why I did - n't come. I don't know why I
G7sus C
did - n't come.
Fine
2.
Am7 D7 G7sus C
catch - ing tear - drops in my hand. My
Am7 D7 G7
heart is drenched in wine, but
Am7 D7 G7
you'll be on my mind for - ev - er.
D.S. al Fine
(take 1st ending)

DON'T STOP BELIEVIN'

HORN

Words and Music by STEVE PERRY,
NEAL SCHON and JONATHAN CAIN

Moderately fast
F C Dm7
Just a small - town girl livin' in a
B♭ F C
lone - ly world. She took the mid - night train go - in'
Am B♭ F
an - y - where. Just a
C Dm7 B♭
cit - y boy born and raised in south De - troit.
F C Am
He took a mid - night train go - in' an - y - where.
B♭ F C
A sing - er in a smok - y room,
Dm7 B♭ F
the smell of wine and cheap per - fume. For a smile they can
C Am B♭
share the night. It goes on and on and on and on.

C/B♭ B♭ C/B♭ F/B♭ C/F F
Stran - gers wait - ing up and down the
C/F F C/B♭ B♭ C/B♭ F/B♭
boul - e - vard, their shad - ows search - ing in the night.
C/F F C/F F C/B♭ B♭
Street - light
C/B♭ F/B♭ C/F F C/F F
peo - ple, liv - ing just to find e - mo - tion,
C/B♭ B♭ C/B♭ F/B♭ C F
hid - ing some - where in the night.
C F B♭ F C
Don't stop be - liev - in'.
Dm7 B♭ F
Hold on to the feel - in'. Street - light
C Am B♭ F
peo - ple.

EDELWEISS

from THE SOUND OF MUSIC

HORN

Lyrics by OSCAR HAMMERSTEIN II
Music by RICHARD RODGERS

Moderately
C G7/B C/E F/A
E - del - weiss, e - del - weiss,
C/G Am7 Dm7 G7
ev - 'ry morn - ing you greet me.
C G7/B C/E F/A
Small and white, clean and bright,
C/G G7 C
you look hap - py to meet me.
G7/B G7 C
Blos - som of snow, may you bloom and grow,
F D7/F♯ G G7
bloom and grow for - ev - er.
C C/B♭ F/A Fm/A♭
E - del - weiss, e - del - weiss,
C/G G7 C
bless my home - land for - ev - er.

EIGHT DAYS A WEEK

HORN

Words and Music by JOHN LENNON
and PAUL McCARTNEY

Moderately fast
G
A
C
G
1., 3. Ooh, I need your love, babe; guess you know it's true.
2. Love you ev - 'ry day, girl; al - ways on my mind.

A
C
G
Hope you need my love, babe, just like I need you.
One thing I can say, girl: love you all the time.

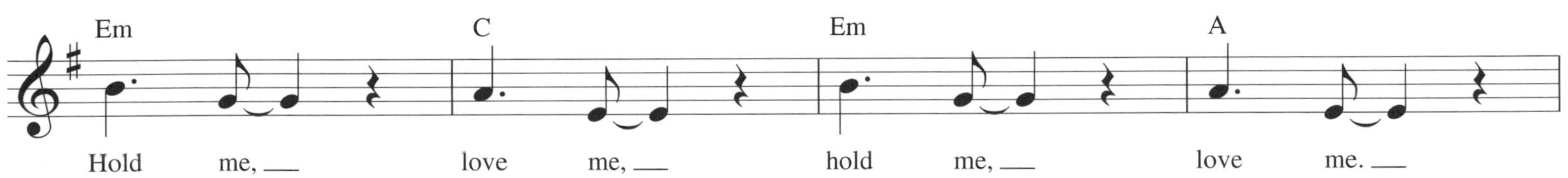
Em
C
Em
A
Hold me, love me, hold me, love me.

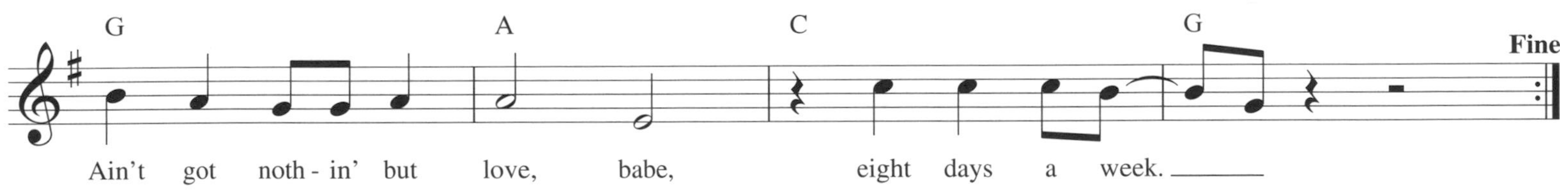
G
A
C
G
Fine
Ain't got noth - in' but love, babe, eight days a week.

D
Em
Eight days a week I love you.

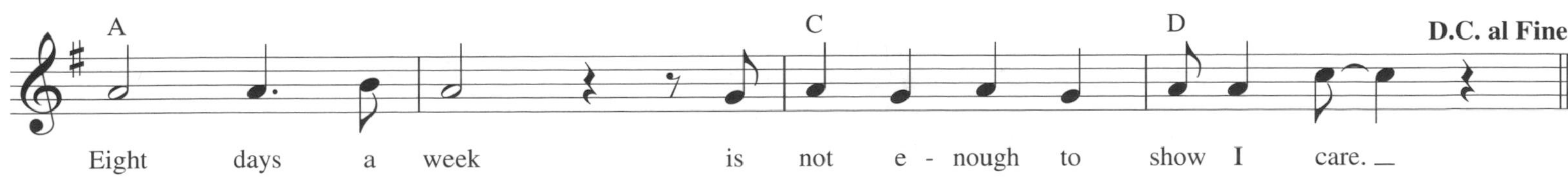
A
C
D
D.C. al Fine
Eight days a week is not e - nough to show I care.

EVERY BREATH YOU TAKE

HORN

Music and Lyrics by
STING

Moderately
N.C.
C
Am
Ev - 'ry breath you __ take,
ev - 'ry move you __ make,
Ev - 'ry move you __ make,
ev - 'ry vow you __ break,

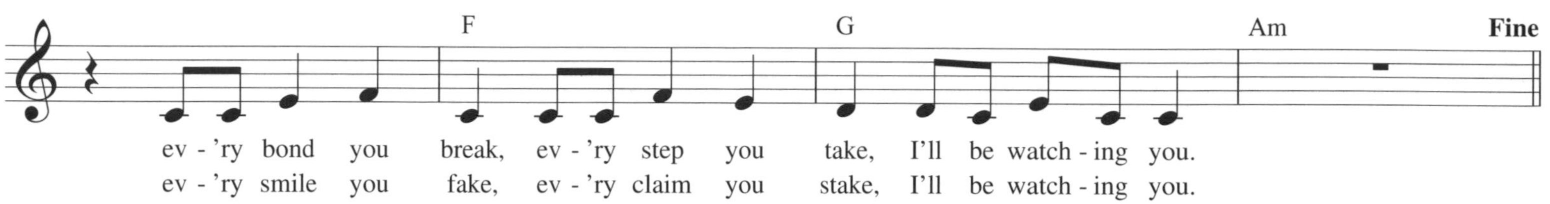
F
G
Am
Fine
ev - 'ry bond you break, ev - 'ry step you take, I'll be watch - ing you.
ev - 'ry smile you fake, ev - 'ry claim you stake, I'll be watch - ing you.

C
Am
Ev - 'ry sin - gle __ day,
ev - 'ry word you __ say,

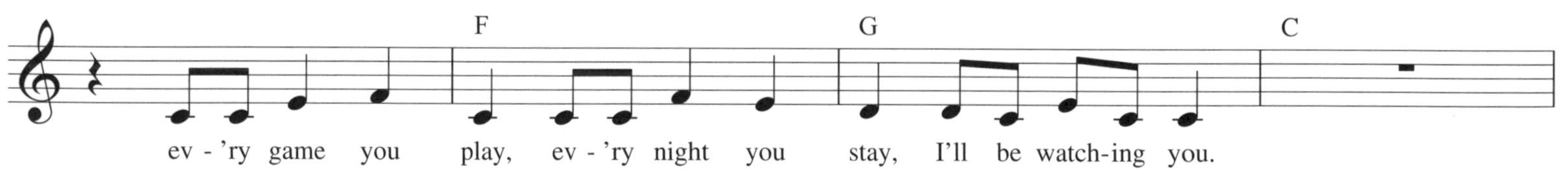
F
G
C
ev - 'ry game you play, ev - 'ry night you stay, I'll be watch-ing you.

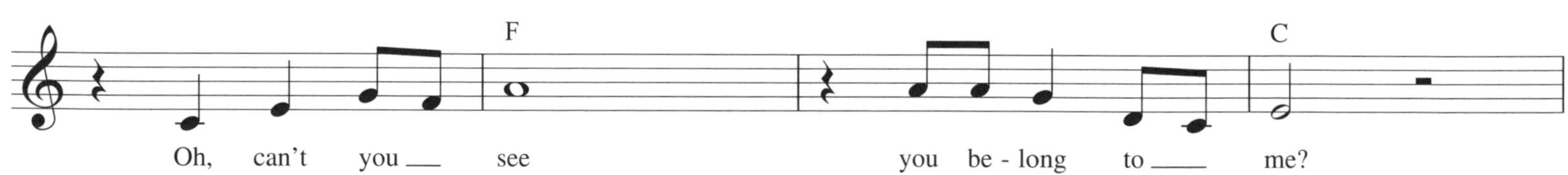
F
C
Oh, can't you __ see
you be - long to __ me?

D
G
D.C. al Fine
How my poor heart _ aches _
with ev - 'ry step __ you take.

FIREFLIES

HORN

Words and Music by
ADAM YOUNG

Moderately fast
C F B♭
You would not be - lieve your eyes if ten mil - lion fi - re - flies
'Cause I get a thou - sand hugs from ten thou - sand light - ning bugs
C F B♭
lit up the world as I fell a - sleep.
as they try to teach me how to dance.
C F B♭
'Cause they fill the o - pen air and leave tear - drops ev - 'ry - where. You'd think
A fox - trot, a - bove my head, a sock - hop be - neath my bed, a dis -
C F B♭
me rude, but I would just stand and stare.
- co ball is just hang - ing by a thread.
C Dm7 Csus
I'd like to make my - self be - lieve that plan - et Earth
B♭ F Am B♭
turns slow - ly. It's
F B♭ C Dm
hard to say that I'd rath - er stay a - wake when I'm a - sleep 'cause
B♭ F 1. G F 2. C
ev - 'ry - thing is nev - er as it seems. seems.

GEORGIA ON MY MIND

HORN

Words by STUART GORRELL
Music by HOAGY CARMICHAEL

Moderately
F A7 Dm Cm6 B♭ Bm7♭5
Geor - gia, Geor - gia, the whole day through. Just an
Geor - gia, Geor - gia, a song of you comes as
F/C D7 Gm7 C7 F F♯dim7 Gm7 C7
1.
old sweet song keeps Geor - gia on my mind.
sweet and clear as
2.
Gm7 C7 F B♭7 F A7 Dm B♭/D
moon - light through the pines. Oth - er arms reach
Bdim/D B♭/D Dm B♭/D Dm7 G7
out to me; oth - er eyes smile ten - der - ly.
Dm B♭/D Dm7 E7 Am7 A♭7♭5 Gm7 C7
Still in peace - ful dreams I see the road leads back to you.
F A7 Dm Cm6 B♭ Bm7♭5
Geor - gia, Geor - gia, no peace I find. Just an
F/C D7 Gm7 C7 F B♭7 F
old sweet song keeps Geor - gia on my mind.

IN MY LIFE

HORN

Words and Music by JOHN LENNON
and PAUL McCARTNEY

Moderately
G D Em G7 C Cm
There are plac - es I re - mem - ber all my life, though
all these friends and lov - ers, there is no one com -
G D Em G7
some have changed. Some for - ev - er, not for bet - ter; some have
pares with you. And these mem - 'ries lose their mean - ing when I
C Cm G Em
gone and some re - main. All these plac - es have their
think of love as some - thing new. Though I know I'll nev - er lose af -
C F G
mo - ments with lov - ers and friends I still can re - call. Some are
fec - tion for peo - ple and things that went be - fore, I
Em A
dead and some are liv - ing. In
know I'll of - ten stop and think a - bout them. In
Cm G
my life I've loved them all.
my life I love you more.
1. D 2. D G
But of

HEY, SOUL SISTER

HORN

Words and Music by PAT MONAHAN,
ESPEN LIND and AMUND BJORKLAND

Moderately

F
C
Dm
Hey,
hey,
hey.

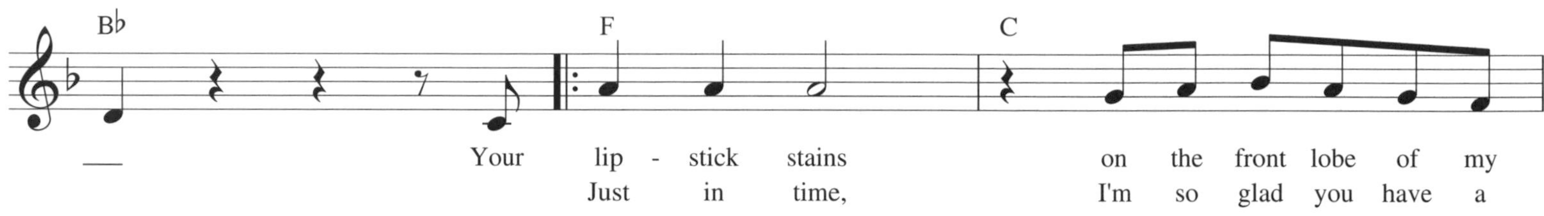
B♭
F
C
Your lip - stick stains on the front lobe of my
Just in time, I'm so glad you have a

Dm
B♭
F
left - side brains. I know I wouldn't for - get ya, and so I went and
one - track mind like me. You gave my life di - rec - tion, a game show love con -

C
Dm
B♭
C
let you blow my mind. Your
nec - tion we can't de - ny. I'm

F
C
Dm
sweet moon - beam, the smell of you in ev - 'ry sin - gle dream I dream.
so ob - sessed; my heart is bound to beat right out my un - trimmed chest.

B♭
F
C
I knew when we col - lid - ed you're the one I have de - cid - ed who's one of my kind.
I be - lieve in you; like a vir - gin, you're Ma - don - na, and I'm al - ways gon - na

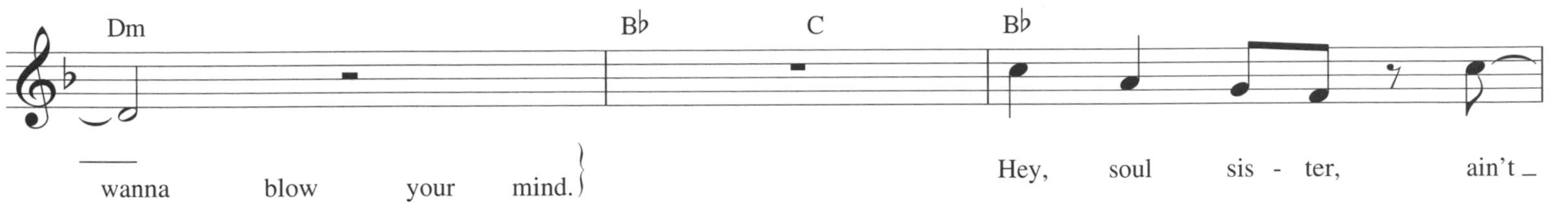
Dm
B♭
C
B♭
wanna blow your mind.
Hey, soul sis - ter, ain't

C
F
C
B♭
C
F
C
that Mis - ter Mis - ter on the ra - di - o, ster - e - o? The way you move ain't fair, you know.

B♭
C
F
C
B♭
Hey, soul sis - ter, I don't wan - na miss a sin - gle thing you do

C
F
C
to - night.
Hey,
hey,

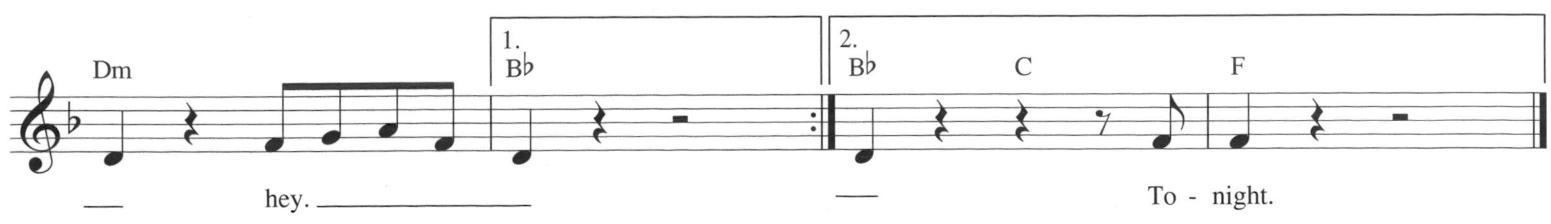
Dm
1.
B♭
2.
B♭
C
F
hey.
To - night.

HOT N COLD

HORN

Words and Music by KATY PERRY,
MAX MARTIN and LUKASZ GOTTWALD

Moderately fast
G
D
Am
You change your mind like a girl chang-es clothes.
We used to be just like twins, so in sync.

C
G
D
Yeah, you P - M - S like a bitch;
The same en - er - gy now's a dead

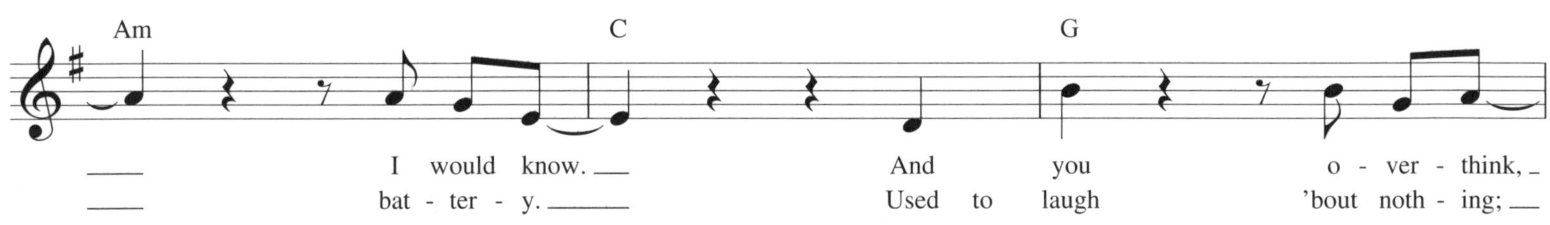
Am
C
G
I would know. And you o - ver - think,
bat - ter - y. Used to laugh 'bout noth - ing;

D
Am
C
al - ways speak cryp - tic - 'ly. I should know
now you're plain bor - ing. I should know

G
D
Am
that you're no good for me.
that you're not gon - na change.

C
G
D
'Cause you're hot then you're cold. You're yes then you're no. You're in

Am
C
G
then you're out. You're up then you're down. You're wrong when it's right. It's black

D
Am
C
and it's white. We fight, we break up. We kiss, we make up.

G
D
Am
You don't real - ly wan - na stay, no, but you don't real - ly wan - na

C
G
D
go. You're hot then you're cold. You're yes then you're no. You're in

Am
1.
C
2.
C
G
then you're out. You're up then you're down. then you're down.

ISN'T SHE LOVELY

HORN

Words and Music by
STEVIE WONDER

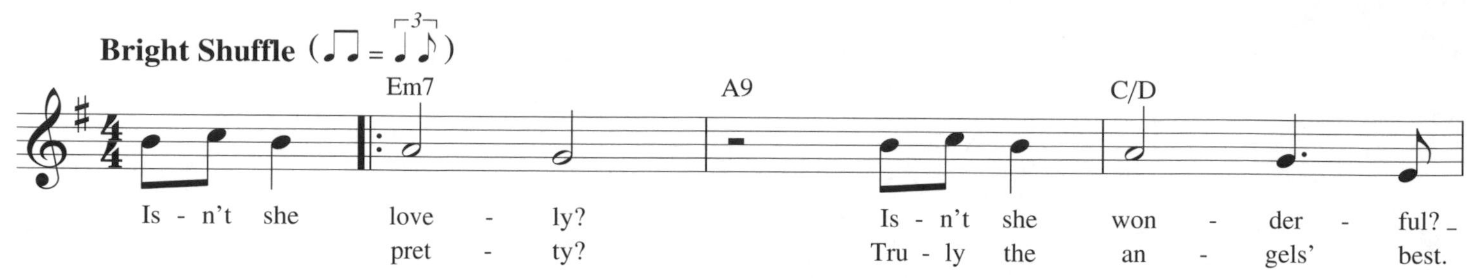
Bright Shuffle
Em7
A9
C/D
Is - n't she love - ly? Is - n't she won - der - ful?
pret - ty? Tru - ly the an - gels' best.

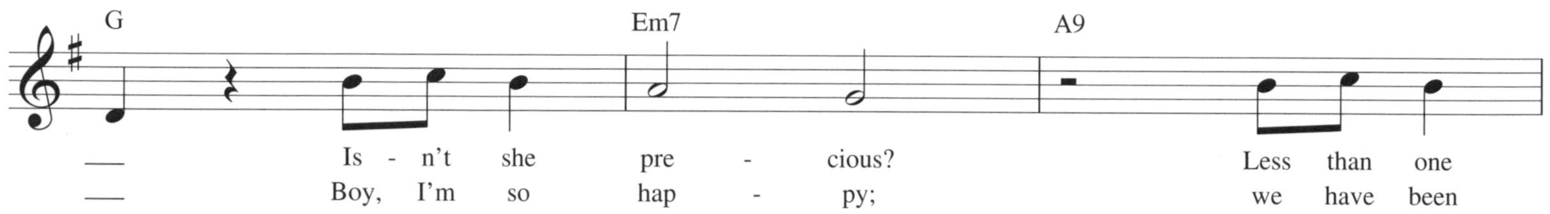
G
Em7
A9
Is - n't she pre - cious? Less than one
Boy, I'm so hap - py; we have been

C/D
G
Cmaj7
min - ute old. I nev - er thought through love we'd be
heav - en blessed. I can't be - lieve what God has done.

B7#5
Em7
A13
mak - ing one as love - ly as she.
Through us He's giv - en life to one.
But is - n't she

C/D
G
1.
2.
love - ly? Made from love. Is - n't she

THE LETTER

HORN

Words and Music by
WAYNE CARSON THOMPSON

Moderately
Em
C
D
1., 3. Give me a tick - et for an aer - o - plane. Ain't got time to take a
2. I don't care how much mon - ey I got - ta spend. Got to get back to my

A
Em
C
fast train.
ba - by again.
Lone - ly days are gone; I'm a - go - in' home. Oh, my

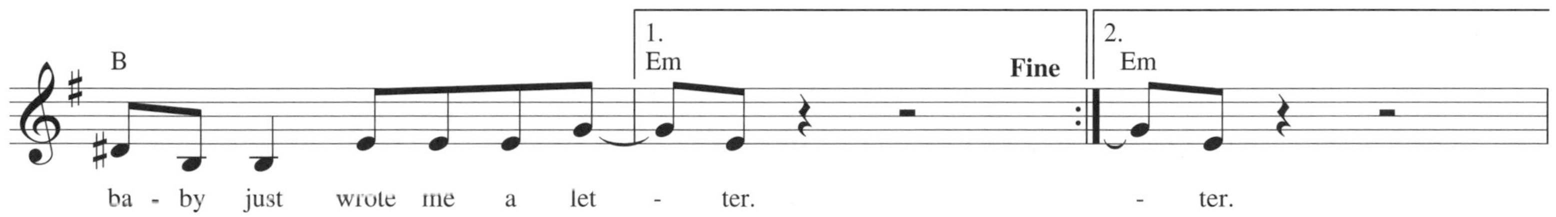
B
1.
Em
Fine
2.
Em
ba - by just wrote me a let - ter. - ter.

G
D
C
G
Well, she wrote me a let - ter, said she could - n't live with - out

D
G
D
me no more. Lis - ten, mis - ter, can't you see I

D.C. al Fine
(take 1st ending)
C
G
D
B
got to get back to my ba - by once more? An - y - way, yeah.

LIKE A VIRGIN

HORN

Words and Music by BILLY STEINBERG
and TOM KELLY

Moderately
G6
I made it through the wil - der-ness. Some-how I made it through.
all my love, boy. My fear is fad - ing fast.
Am7
Did - n't know how lost I was un - til I
Been sav - ing it all for you 'cause on - ly
G6
found you. I was beat, in - com - plete. I'd been had;
love can last. You're so fine and you're mine. Make me strong;
Am7
I was sad and blue. But you made me feel,
yeah, you make me bold. Oh, your loved thawed out,
Em7 Am7 Em7
yeah, you made me feel shin - y and new.
yeah, your love thawed out what was scared and cold.
Dsus D Dsus2 D G6
Like a vir - gin touched for the
Like a vir - gin touched for the
Am7
ver - y first time. Like a vir - gin when your
ver - y first time. Like a vir - gin with your
G6
1. 2.
heart beats next to mine. Gonna give you
heart - beat next to mine.

THE LOOK OF LOVE

from CASINO ROYALE

HORN

Words by HAL DAVID
Music by BURT BACHARACH

Moderately
Dm7(add4) Am9
The look of love is in your eyes, the look
of love; it's on your face, a look
Bbmaj7b5 Bb6 A7sus A7
your heart can't dis - guise. The look
that time can't e - rase. Be mine
Dm7(add4) D7sus D7 Bbmaj7 Bbm(maj7)
of love is say - ing so much more than just
to - night; let this be just the start of so
Fmaj7 F7 Bbmaj7
words could ev - er say. And what my heart has heard, well, it
man - y nights like this. Let's take a lov - er's vow and then
A7sus A7 Dm7 G7 Fmaj7
takes my breath a - way. I can hard - ly wait to hold you, feel
seal it with a kiss.
Gm7/C Fmaj7
my arms a - round you. How long I have wait - ed, wait - ed just to love you, now
Gm7/C 1. 2. Dm7
that I have found you. You've got the look Don't ev - er go.
G9 Gm7 Gm7/C F6
Don't ev - er go. rit. I love you so.

LOVE ME TENDER

HORN

Words and Music by ELVIS PRESLEY
and VERA MATSON

Moderately
G
A7
D7
Love me ten - der, love me sweet; nev - er let me
Love me ten - der, love me long; take me to your

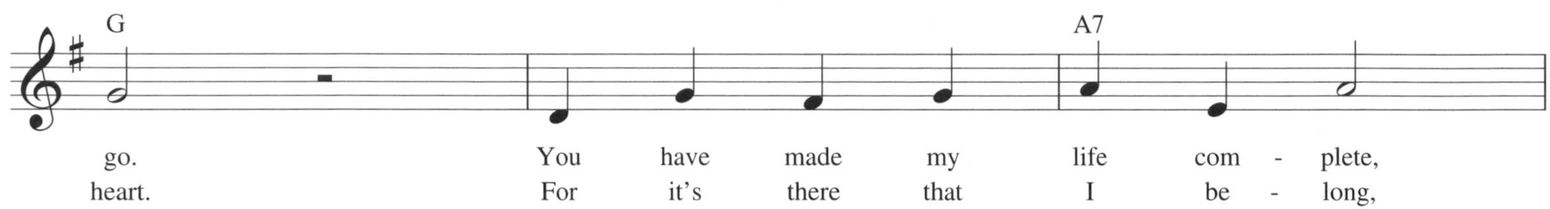
G
A7
go. You have made my life com - plete,
heart. For it's there that I be - long,

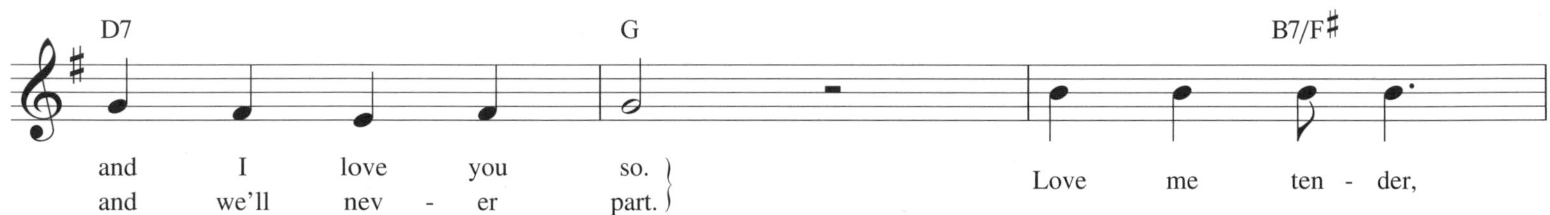
D7
G
B7/F♯
and I love you so.
and we'll nev - er part.
Love me ten - der,

Em
G7/D
C
Cm
G
love me true. All my dreams ful - fill.

E7
A7
1.
D7
For, my dar - ling, I love you, and I al - ways

G
2.
D7
G
will. and I al - ways will.

MR. TAMBOURINE MAN

HORN

Words and Music by
BOB DYLAN

Moderately fast
F G C F
Hey, Mis - ter Tam - bou - rine Man, play a song for me. I'm not
C F G
sleep - y and there is no place I'm go - ing to.
F G C F
Hey, Mis - ter Tam - bou - rine Man, play a song for me. In the
C F G C
Fine
jin - gle jan - gle morn - ing I'll come fol - low - ing you.
F G C
Though I know this eve - ning's em - pire has re - turned in - to
wea - ri - ness a - maz - es me. I'm brand - ed on my
F C F C
sand, van - ished from my hand, left me blind - ly here to
feet. I have no one to meet, and the an - cient emp - ty
F G
1.
2.
D.C. al Fine
stand but still not sleep - ing, my
street's too dead for dream - ing.

LOVE STORY

HORN

Words and Music by
TAYLOR SWIFT

Moderately
G
C
We were both young when I first saw _ you. I close my eyes _ and the

Em
C
flash-back starts. _ I'm stand-ing there on a bal-co-ny in sum-mer air.

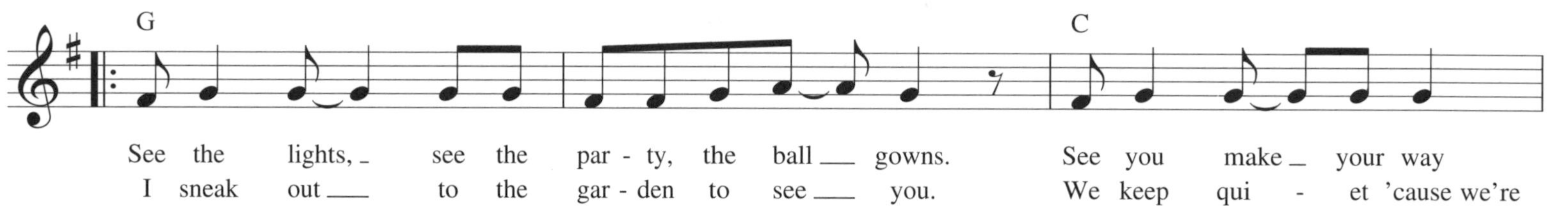
G
C
See the lights, _ see the par - ty, the ball _ gowns. See you make _ your way
I sneak out _ to the gar - den to see _ you. We keep qui - et 'cause we're

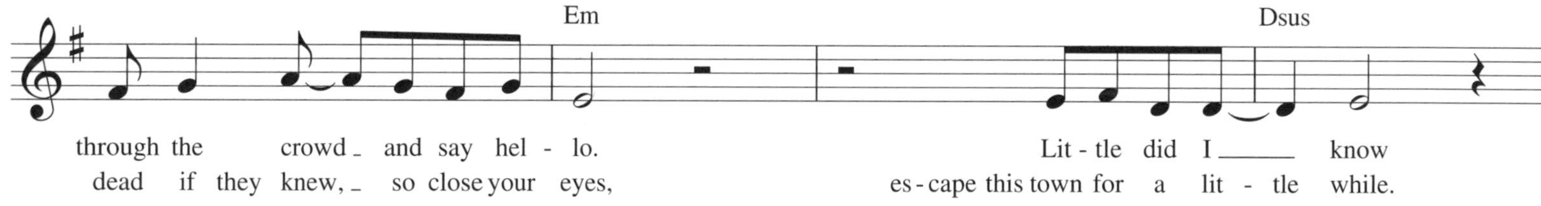
Em
Dsus
through the crowd _ and say hel - lo. Lit - tle did I _ know
dead if they knew, _ so close your eyes, es - cape this town for a lit - tle while.

C
Dsus
that you were Ro - me - o. You were throw - ing peb - bles, and my
'Cause you were Ro - me - o; I was the scar - let let - ter. And my

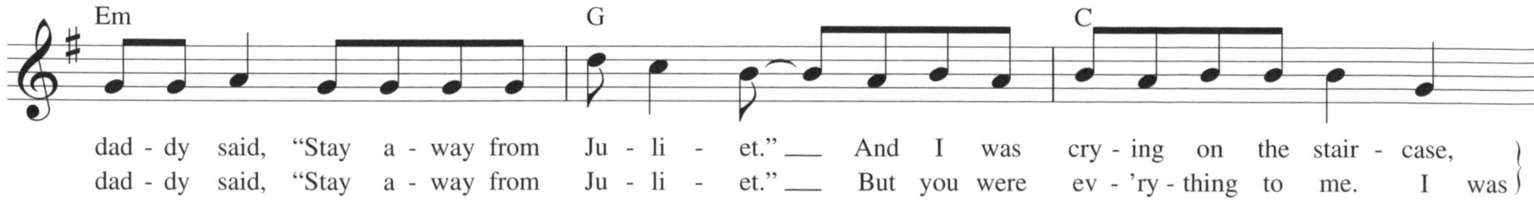
Em
G
C
dad - dy said, "Stay a - way from Ju - li - et." _ And I was cry - ing on the stair - case,
dad - dy said, "Stay a - way from Ju - li - et." _ But you were ev - 'ry - thing to me. I was

Copyright © 2008 Sony/ATV Music Publishing LLC and Taylor Swift Music
All Rights Administered by Sony/ATV Music Publishing LLC, 8 Music Square West, Nashville, TN 37203
International Copyright Secured All Rights Reserved

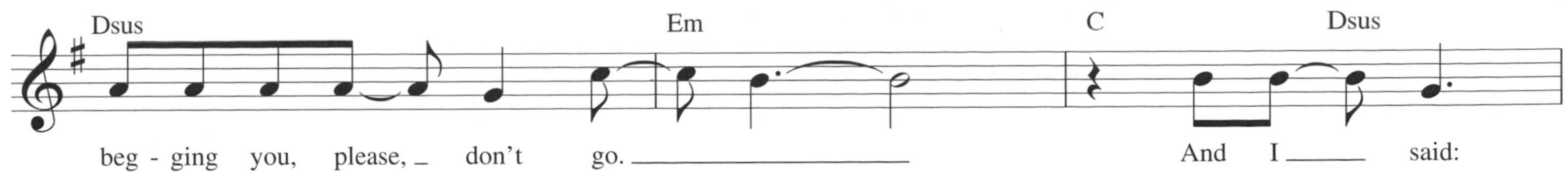
Dsus
Em
C
Dsus
beg - ging you, please, don't go.
And I said:

G
Dsus
Ro - me - o, take me some-where we can be a - lone. I'll be wait - ing.

Em
All there's left to do is run. You'll be the prince and I'll be the prin - cess.

C
1.
Dsus
N.C.
G
It's a love sto - ry. Ba - by, just say yes.
So

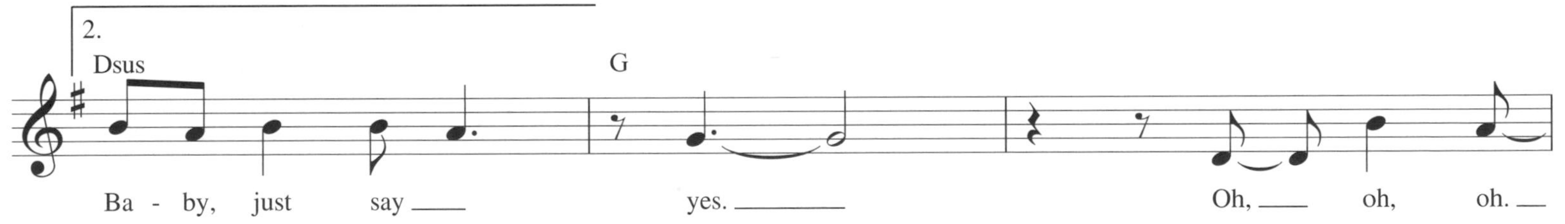
2.
Dsus
G
Ba - by, just say yes.
Oh, oh, oh.

D
Em
Oh, oh, oh, oh.

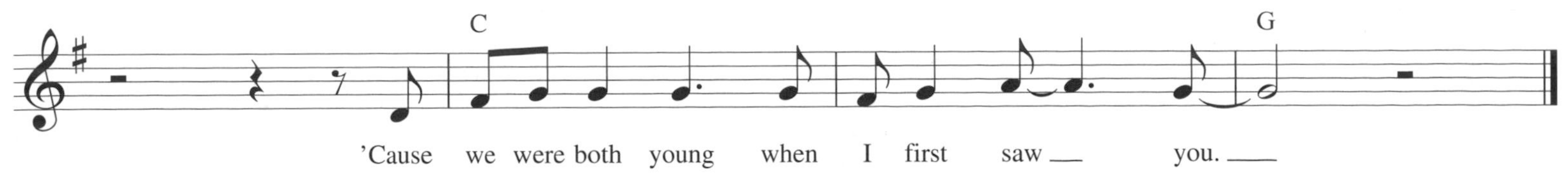
C
G
'Cause we were both young when I first saw you.

MOON RIVER

from the Paramount Picture BREAKFAST AT TIFFANY'S

HORN

Words by JOHNNY MERCER
Music by HENRY MANCINI

Moderately
C Am F C/E
Moon Riv - er, wid - er than a mile. I'm
F C/E Bm7♭5 E7 Am
cross - ing you in style some - day. Old dream
C7/G F B♭9♭5 Am
mak - er, you heart - break - er, wher - ev - er you're
F♯m7♭5 B7 Em7 A7 Dm7 G7 C Am
go - ing, I'm go - ing your way. Two drift - ers,
F C/E F C/E Bm7♭5
off to see the world. There's such a lot of world to see.
E7 Am Am/G F♯m7♭5 F7
We're af - ter the same rain - bow's
C/E F C/E F C/E
end wait - ing 'round the bend, my huck - le - ber - ry friend,
Am Dm G7 C
Moon Riv - er and me.

MORNING HAS BROKEN

HORN

Words by ELEANOR FARJEON
Music by CAT STEVENS

Moderately
C Dm G
Morn - ing has bro - ken, like the first morn - ing.
new fall, sun - lit from heav - en,
F C Em
Black - bird has spo - ken, like the first bird.
like the first dew - fall on the first grass.
Am D G
C F C
Praise for the sing - ing, praise for the morn - ing.
Praise for the sweet - ness of the wet gar - den,
Am D G C
Praise for the spring - ing, fresh from the world.
sprung in com - plete - ness where his feet pass.
F G C F
1. G7sus
Sweet the rain's
2. G C

MY CHERIE AMOUR

HORN

Words and Music by STEVIE WONDER,
SYLVIA MOY and HENRY COSBY

Moderately
Gmaj7 C7sus C7
My che - rie a - mour, love - ly as a sum - mer day.
ca - fé, or some - times on a crowd - ed street,
Fmaj7 D7sus D7 Gmaj7 C7sus C7
My che - rie a - mour, dis - tant as the Milk - y Way.
I've been near you, but you nev - er no - ticed me.
Fmaj7 D7sus D7 Cmaj7 D7sus D7
My che - rie a - mour, pret - ty lit - tle one that I
My che - rie a - mour, won't you tell me, how could you
F9♭5 E7 A9
a - dore, you're the on - ly girl my heart beats for;
ig - nore that be - hind that lit - tle smile I wore,
D7 Gmaj7 1. D13♭9 2. D13♭9
how I wish that you were mine. In a La la
Cmaj7 Fmaj7 Gmaj7
la la la la, la la la la la la. La la
Cmaj7 Fmaj7 Gmaj7
la la la la, la la la la la la.

MY GIRL

HORN

Words and Music by WILLIAM "SMOKEY" ROBINSON
and RONALD WHITE

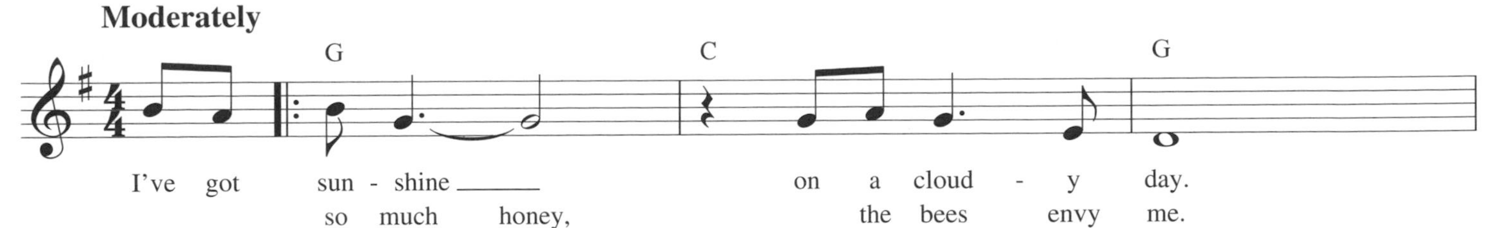
Moderately
G
C
G
I've got sun - shine on a cloud - y day.
so much honey, the bees envy me.

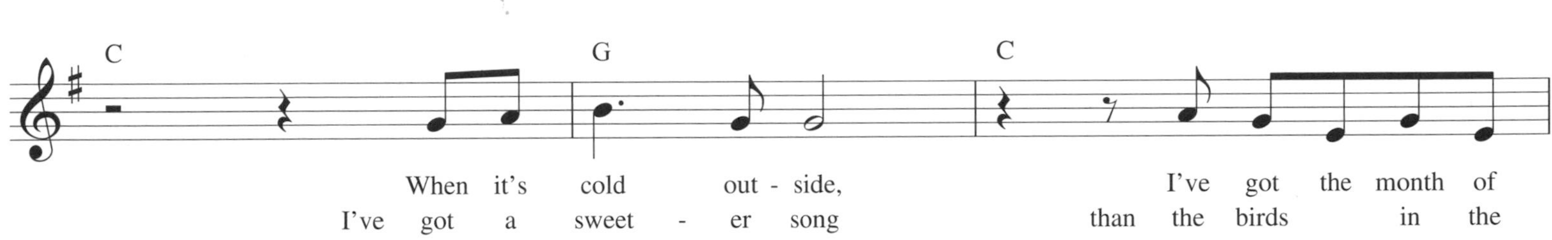
C
G
C
When it's cold out - side, I've got the month of
I've got a sweet - er song than the birds in the

G
C
G Am
C D
G Am
May.
trees.
I guess you say, what can make me

C D
G
feel this way? My girl. (My girl, my girl.) Talk - in' 'bout

Am7
1.
D7
2.
D7 G
my girl. (My girl.) I've got (My girl.)

MY FAVORITE THINGS

from THE SOUND OF MUSIC

HORN

Lyrics by OSCAR HAMMERSTEIN II
Music by RICHARD RODGERS

Brightly

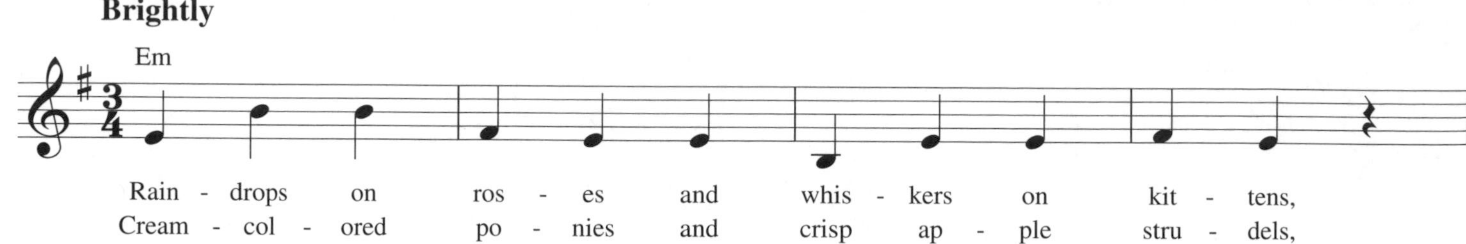
Em
Rain - drops on ros - es and whis - kers on kit - tens,
Cream - col - ored po - nies and crisp ap - ple stru - dels,

Cmaj7
bright cop - per ket - tles and warm wool - en mit - tens,
door - bells and sleigh - bells and schnit - zel with noo - dles,

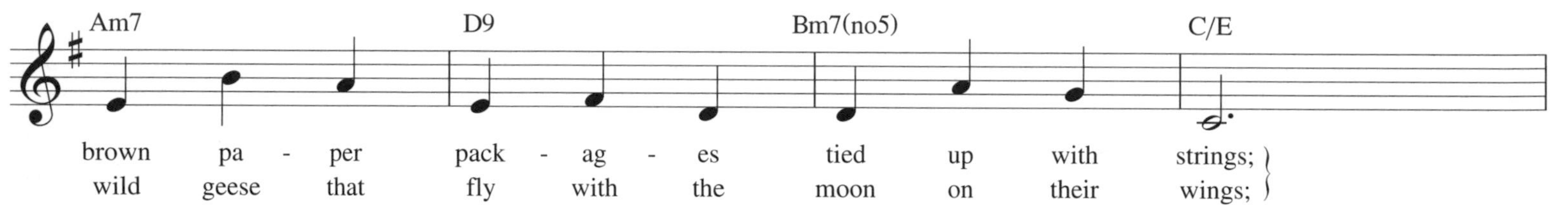
Am7
D9
Bm7(no5)
C/E
brown pa - per pack - ag - es tied up with strings;
wild geese that fly with the moon on their wings;

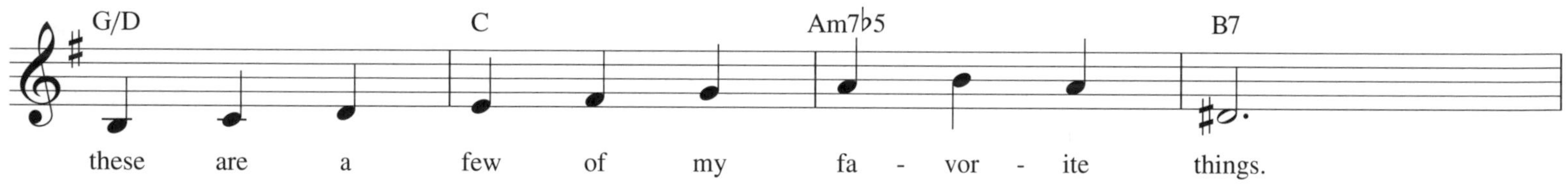
G/D
C
Am7♭5
B7
these are a few of my fa - vor - ite things.

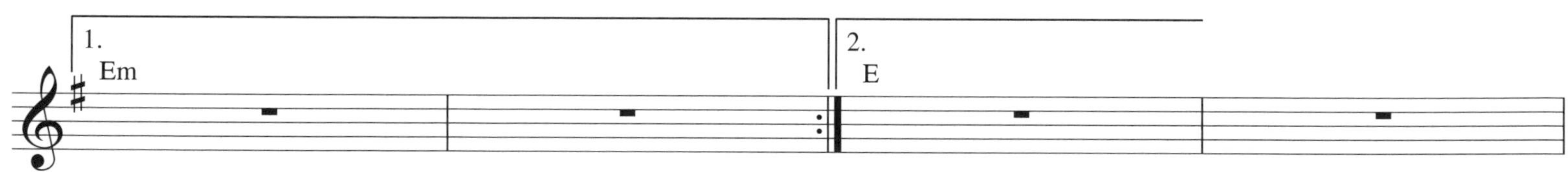
1.
Em
2.
E

Girls in white dress - es with blue sat - in sash - es,

A
snow - flakes that stay on my nose and eye - lash - es,
Am7 D9 Bm7(no5) C/E
sil - ver white win - ters that melt in - to springs;
G/D C F#m7b5 B7b9
these are a few of my fa - vor - ite things.
Em F#m7b5 B7
When the dog bites, when the bee stings,
Em C
when I'm feel - ing sad, I
A7
sim - ply re - mem - ber my fa - vor - ite things and
G/D C D7b9 D7
then I don't feel so
G C G
bad.

MY HEART WILL GO ON

(Love Theme from 'Titanic')

from the Paramount and Twentieth Century Fox Motion Picture TITANIC

HORN

Music by JAMES HORNER
Lyric by WILL JENNINGS

Moderately
G D C G/D D
Ev - 'ry night in my dreams, I see you, I feel you.
Love can touch us one time and last for a life - time
G D C
This is how I know you go on.
and nev - er let go till we're gone.
G D C G/D D
Far a - cross the dis - tance and spac - es be - tween us,
Love was when I loved you, one true time I hold to.
G D C
you have come to show you go on.
In my life we'll al - ways go on.
Em D C D Em
Near, far, wher - ev - er you are I be - lieve that the
D C D Em D
heart does go on. Once more you
C D Em Bm C
o - pen the door and you're here in my heart, and my heart will go
D 1. Em D 2. G
on and on. on.

NIGHTS IN WHITE SATIN

HORN

Words and Music by
JUSTIN HAYWARD

Moderately fast
Dm
C
Dm
Nights in white sat - in,
nev - er reach - ing the
Gaz - ing at peo - ple,
some hand in
C
B♭
F
end.
Let - ters I've writ - ten,
hand.
Just what I'm go - ing through,
E♭
Dm
nev - er mean - ing to send.
Beau - ty I'd
they can't un - der - stand.
Some try to
C
Dm
C
al - ways missed
with these eyes be - fore.
tell me
thoughts they can - not de - fend.
B♭
F
E♭
Just what the truth is,
I can't say an - y -
Just what you want to be,
you'll be in the
Dm
G
more.
'Cause I
love you,
yes, I
end.
And I
B♭
Dm
love you.
Oh, how I love you.
C
Dm
1.
C
2.

© Copyright 1967 (Renewed), 1968 (Renewed) and 1970 (Renewed) Tyler Music Ltd., London, England
TRO - Essex Music, Inc., New York, controls all publication rights for the U.S.A. and Canada
International Copyright Secured
All Rights Reserved Including Public Performance For Profit
Used by Permission

NOWHERE MAN

HORN

Words and Music by JOHN LENNON
and PAUL McCARTNEY

Moderately
C G F
He's a real no - where man, sit - ting in his
Does - n't have a point of view, knows not where he's
C Dm Fm
no - where land, mak - ing all his no - where plans for
go - ing to. Is - n't he a bit like you and
1. C
no - bod - y.
2. C
me? No-where man,
Em F Em F
please lis - ten. You don't know what you're miss - ing. No-where
Em Dm G
man, the world is at your com - mand.
C G F C
He's a real no - where man, sit - ting in his no - where land,
Dm Fm C
mak - ing all his no - where plans for no - bod - y,
Dm Fm C
mak - ing all his no - where plans for no - bod - y.

PUFF THE MAGIC DRAGON

HORN

Words and Music by LENNY LIPTON
and PETER YARROW

Moderately
C Em F
Puff the Mag - ic Drag - on lived by the
Lit - tle Jack - ie Pa - per loved that ras - cal
C F C Am
sea and frol - icked in the au - tumn mist in a
Puff and brought him strings and seal - ing wax and
1. D G 2. D G
land called Hon - a - lee. oth - er fan - cy
C G C Em
stuff. Oh! Puff the Mag - ic Drag - on
F C F
lived by the sea and frol - icked in the
C Am 1. D G
au - tumn mist in a land called Hon - a - lee.
2. D G C
land called Hon - a - lee.

RAINDROPS KEEP FALLIN' ON MY HEAD

from BUTCH CASSIDY AND THE SUNDANCE KID

HORN

Lyric by HAL DAVID
Music by BURT BACHARACH

Moderate Shuffle
F Fmaj7 F7
Rain - drops keep fall - in' on my head, and just like the guy whose feet are
did me some talk - in' to the sun, and I said I did - n't like the
Rain - drops keep fall - in' on my head, but that does - n't mean my eyes will
B♭maj7 Am7 D9 Am7 D9
too big for his bed, noth - in' seems to fit. Those
way he got things done, sleep - in' on the job. Those
soon be turn - in' red. Cry - in's not for me 'cause
To Coda
Gm7 1. C7sus C7
rain - drops are fall - in' on my head, they keep fall - in'. So I just
rain - drops are fall - in' on my head, they keep fall - in'.
I'm nev - er gon - na stop the rain by com - plain - in'.
2. C7sus C7 F C B B♭
But there's one thing I know: the blues they send to meet
C Am7
me won't de - feat me. It won't be long till
D.C. al Coda
D7 Gm7 N.C. B♭/C C N.C. B♭/C C
hap - pi - ness steps up to greet me.
CODA
C7sus C7 F Fmaj7 Gm7 C7sus F
Be - cause I'm free, noth - in's wor - ry - in' me.

SCARBOROUGH FAIR/CANTICLE

HORN

Arrangement and Original Counter Melody by PAUL SIMON
and ARTHUR GARFUNKEL

Moderately fast
Dm
C
Dm
1., 3. Are you go - ing to Scar - bor - ough Fair?
2. Tell her to make me a cam - bric shirt.
F
Dm
F
G
Pars - ley, sage, rose - mar - y and
Pars - ley, sage, rose - mar - y and
Dm
thyme.
Re -
thyme.
With -
F
C
mem - ber me to one who lives there.
out no seam nor nee - dle - work.
Dm
C
She once was a true love of
Then she'll be a true love of
Dm
1., 2.
3.
mine.
mine.

SOMEWHERE OUT THERE

from AN AMERICAN TAIL

HORN

Music by BARRY MANN and JAMES HORNER
Lyric by CYNTHIA WEIL

Moderately

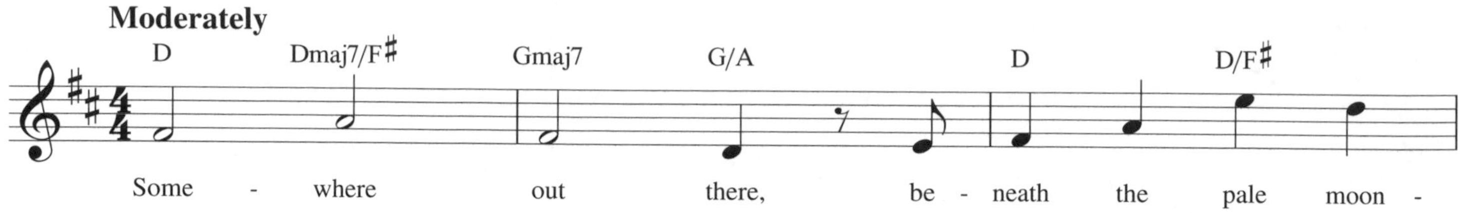
D
Dmaj7/F♯
Gmaj7
G/A
D
D/F♯
Some - where out there, be - neath the pale moon -

G
Em7
A/G
F♯m7
Bm7
light, some - one's think - ing of me and

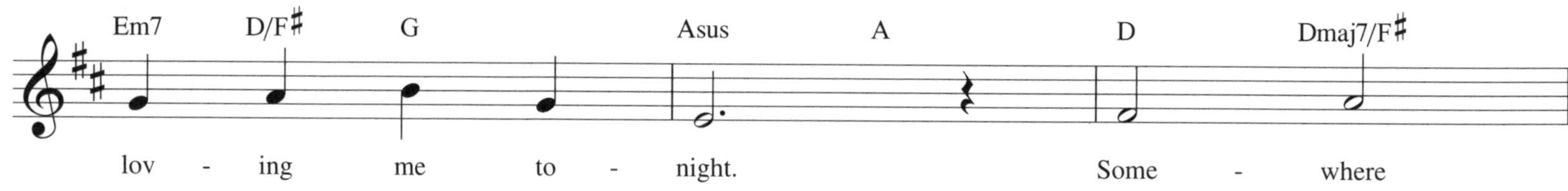
Em7
D/F♯
G
Asus
A
D
Dmaj7/F♯
lov - ing me to - night. Some - where

Gmaj7
G/A
D
D/F♯
G
out there, some - one's say - ing a prayer that

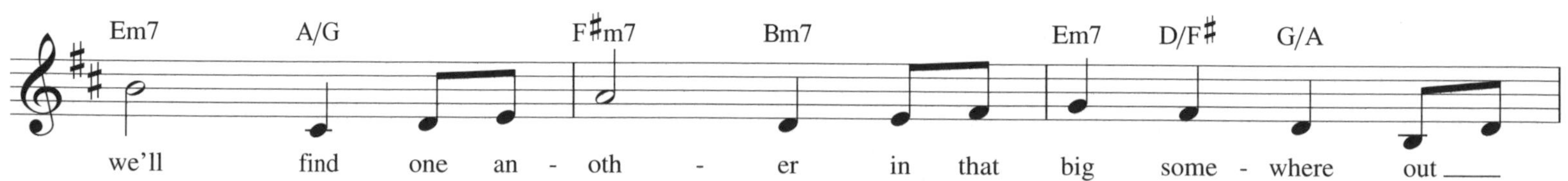
Em7
A/G
F♯m7
Bm7
Em7
D/F♯
G/A
we'll find one an - oth - er in that big some - where out

D
G
A/G
G
A/G
there. And e - ven though I know how ver - y far a - part we are, it

G
A/G
G
A/G
helps to think we might be wish - ing on the same bright star. And

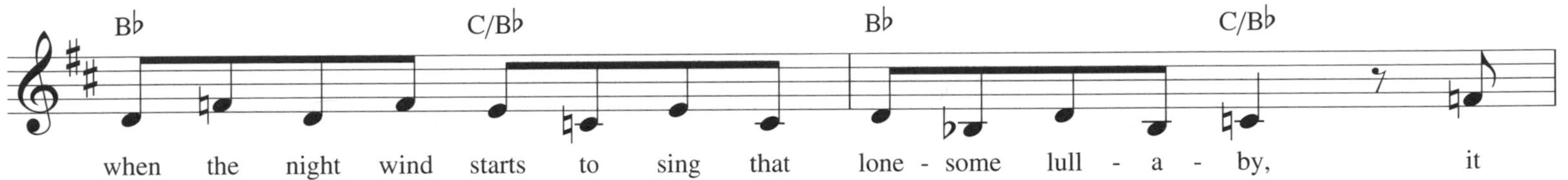
B♭
C/B♭
B♭
C/B♭
when the night wind starts to sing that lone - some lull - a - by, it

B♭
C/B♭
A
helps to think we're sleep - ing un - der - neath the same big sky.

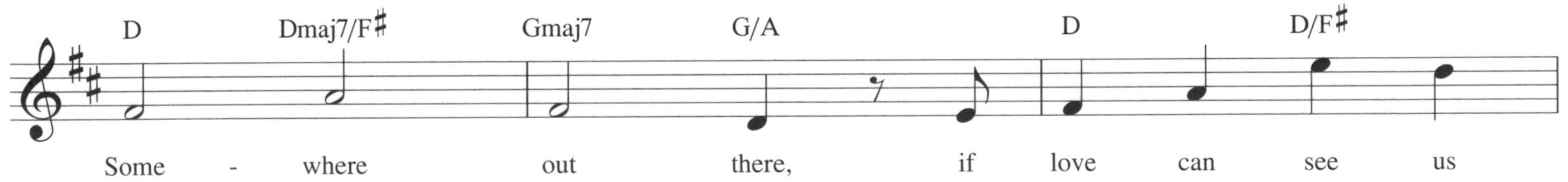
D
Dmaj7/F♯
Gmaj7
G/A
D
D/F♯
Some - where out there, if love can see us

G
Em7
A/G
F♯m7
Bm7
through, then we'll be to - geth - er some - where

G
A
D
out there, out where dreams come true.

THE SOUND OF MUSIC

from THE SOUND OF MUSIC

HORN

Lyrics by OSCAR HAMMERSTEIN II
Music by RICHARD RODGERS

Moderately

F
E/F
The hills are a - live with the sound of mu - sic, with

F
B♭/D
C7
songs they have sung for a thou - sand years. The

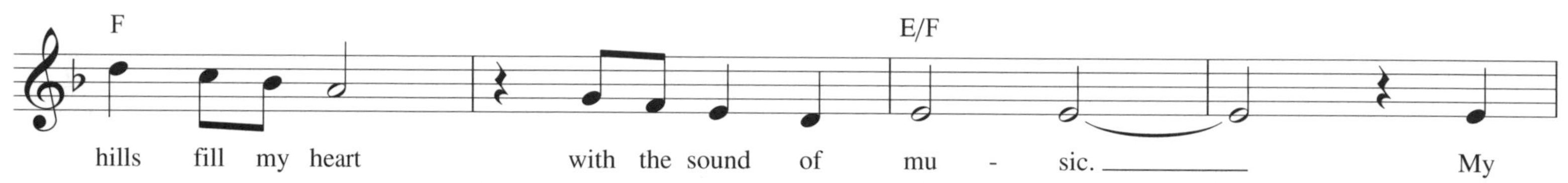
F
E/F
hills fill my heart with the sound of mu - sic. My

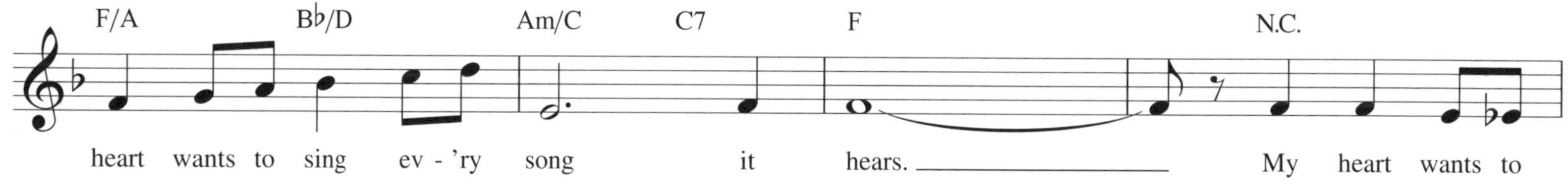
F/A
B♭/D
Am/C
C7
F
N.C.
heart wants to sing ev - 'ry song it hears. My heart wants to

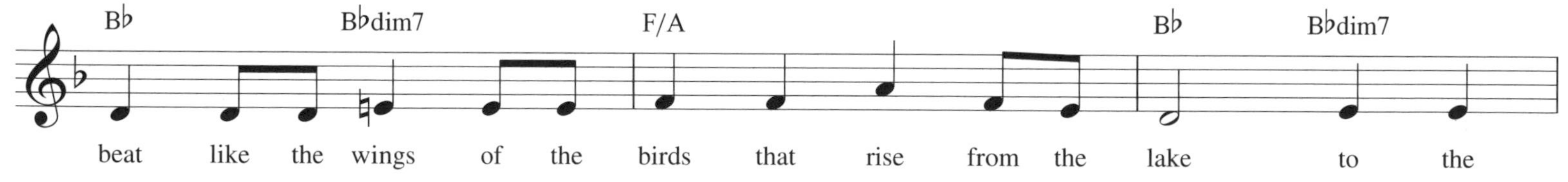
B♭
B♭dim7
F/A
B♭
B♭dim7
beat like the wings of the birds that rise from the lake to the

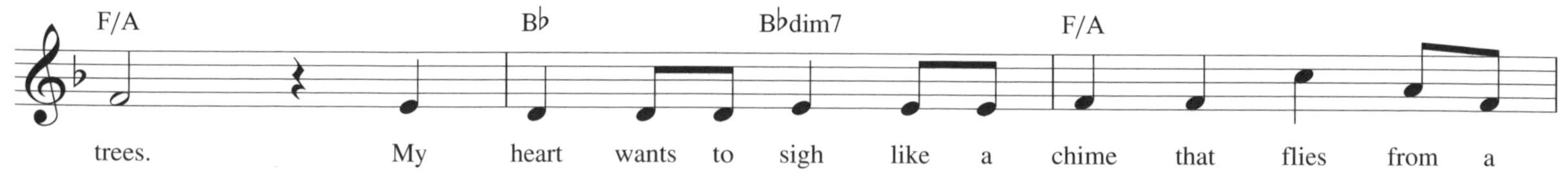
F/A
B♭
B♭dim7
F/A
trees. My heart wants to sigh like a chime that flies from a

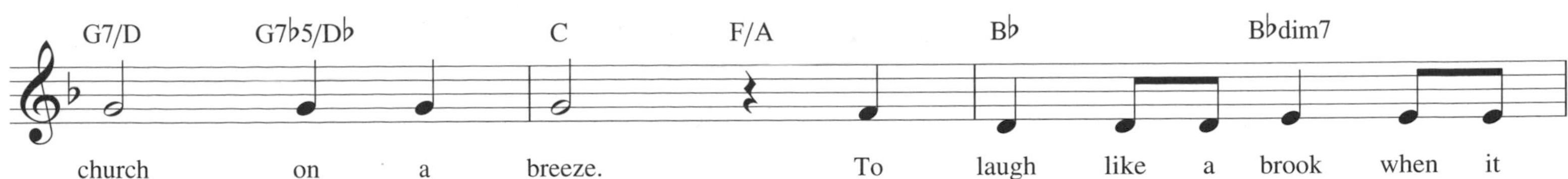
G7/D
G7♭5/D♭
C
F/A
B♭
B♭dim7
church on a breeze. To laugh like a brook when it

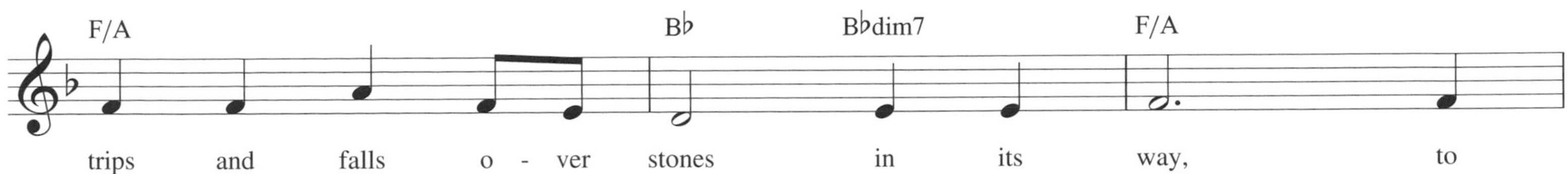
F/A
B♭
B♭dim7
F/A
trips and falls o - ver stones in its way, to

Dm
Am
Dm
G7
C
C7
sing through the night like a lark who is learn - ing to pray. I

F
E/F
go to the hills when my heart is lone - ly. I

F
B♭/D
B♭m/D♭
know I will hear what I've heard be - fore. My

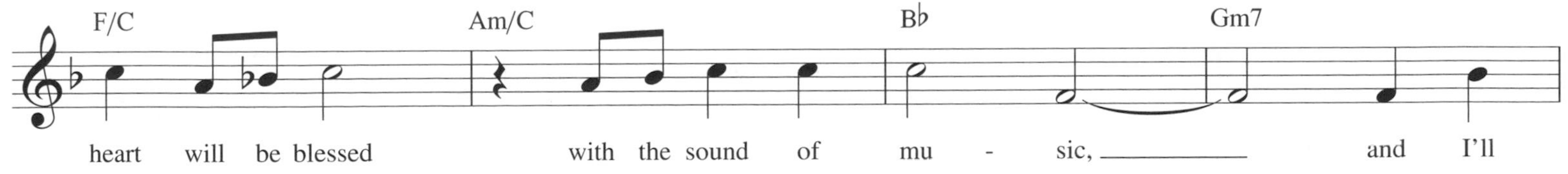
F/C
Am/C
B♭
Gm7
heart will be blessed with the sound of mu - sic, and I'll

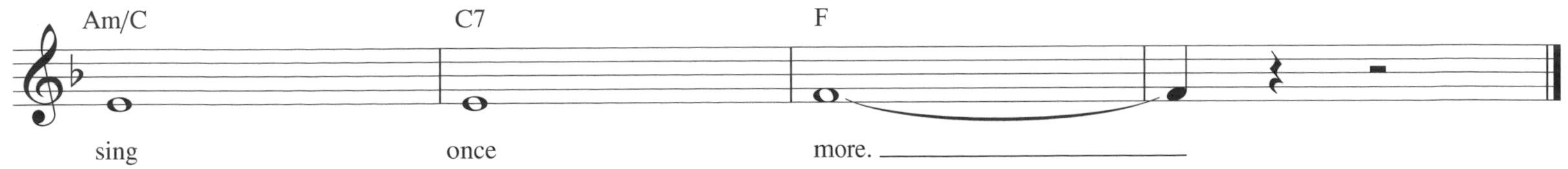
Am/C
C7
F
sing once more.

STRANGERS IN THE NIGHT

adapted from A MAN COULD GET KILLED

HORN

Words by CHARLES SINGLETON and EDDIE SNYDER
Music by BERT KAEMPFERT

Moderately
G
Stran-gers in the night ex-chang-ing glanc - es, won-d'ring in the night what were the chanc - es
Gdim/B♭
Am
we'd be shar - ing love be - fore the night was through.
Some-thing in your eyes was so in - vit - ing, some-thing in your smile was so ex - cit - ing,
D7sus
D7
G
some-thing in my heart told me I must have you.
Bm7♭5
E7♭9
Stran-gers in the night, two lone-ly peo-ple, we were stran-gers in the night up to the mo-ment when we
Am
Am7♭5
G/D
Em7
said our first hel - lo. Lit - tle did we know love was just a glance a - way, a
Am7
D7
G
warm em - brac-ing dance a - way. And ev - er since that night we've been to-geth - er, lov-ers at first sight
Am
D7
G
in love for-ev - er. It turned out so right for stran-gers in the night.

SUNSHINE ON MY SHOULDERS

HORN

Words by JOHN DENVER
Music by JOHN DENVER, MIKE TAYLOR
and DICK KNISS

Moderately
G C G C G C
Sun - shine on my shoul - ders makes me hap - py.
Sun - shine on the wat - er looks so love - ly.
G C G C 1. G C Am7
Sun - shine in my eyes can make me cry.
Sun - shine al - most
D 2. G C To Coda G C G C
al - ways makes me high.
G Am7 Bm C G Am7 Bm C
If I had a day that I could give you, I'd
If I had a song that I could sing for you, I'd
G Am7 1. Bm C Am7 D
give to you a day just like to - day.
sing a song to
2. Bm C G Am7 Bm C
make you feel this way.
D.C. al Coda (take repeat)
CODA
G C G

SWEET CAROLINE

HORN

Words and Music by
NEIL DIAMOND

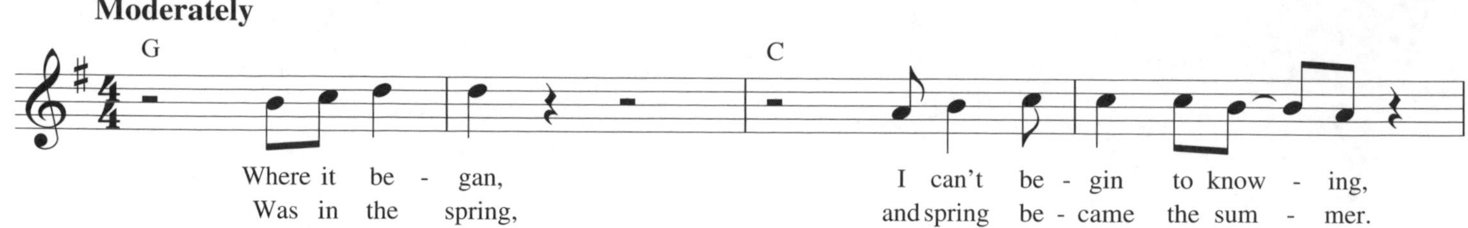
Moderately
G
C
Where it be - gan,
I can't be - gin to know - ing,
Was in the spring,
and spring be - came the sum - mer.

G
1.
D
but then, I know it's grow - ing strong.
Who'd have be - lieved you'd come a -

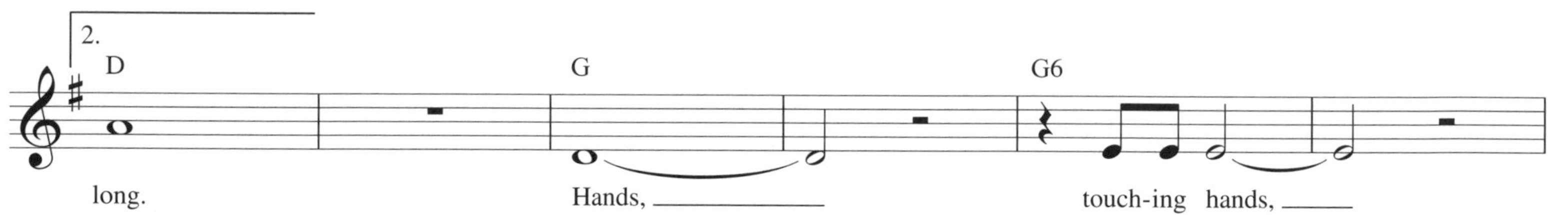
2.
D
G
G6
long.
Hands,
touch-ing hands,

D7
C
D
reach-ing out,
touch-ing me,
touch-ing you.

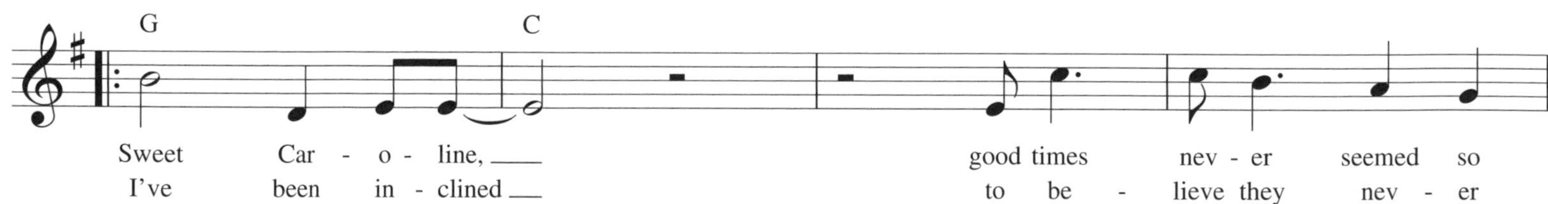
G
C
Sweet Car - o - line,
good times nev - er seemed so
I've been in - clined
to be - lieve they nev - er

1.
D
2.
D
C
Bm
Am
G
good.
would. Oh, no, no.

TILL THERE WAS YOU

from Meredith Willson's THE MUSIC MAN

HORN

By MEREDITH WILLSON

Moderately
C
C♯dim7
Dm7
There were bells on the hills, but I nev - er heard them
birds in the sky, but I nev - er saw them
Fm6
C/G
B/G
Dm7
G7♭9
ring - ing. No, I nev - er heard them at all till there was
wing - ing. No, I nev - er saw them at all till there was
1.
C
Am7
Dm7
G7
you. There were
2.
C
Fmaj7
C
you. And there was
F
F♯dim7
C/G
A7
mu - sic and there were won - der - ful ros - es, they tell me, in
Dm7
D7
G7
G7♯5
sweet fra - grant mead - ows of dawn and dew. There was
C
C♯dim7
Dm7
Fm6
love all a - round, but I nev - er heard it sing - ing. No, I
C/G
B/G
Dm7
G7♭9
C
Fmaj7
C
nev - er heard it at all till there was you.

THE TIMES THEY ARE A-CHANGIN'

HORN

Words and Music by
BOB DYLAN

Moderately fast
F
Dm
B♭
F
Come gath - er 'round, peo - ple, wher - ev - er you roam,
writ - ers and crit - ics who prophe-size with your pen,
Dm
B♭
and ad - mit that the wa - ters a - round you have
and keep your eyes wide; the chance won't come a -
C
F
Dm
B♭
grown, and ac - cept it that soon you'll be drenched to the
gain. And don't speak too soon, for the wheel's still in
F
Gm
bone. If your time to you is worth
spin. And there's no tell - in' who that it's
C
C/B♭
sav - in', then you bet - ter start swim - ming or you'll
nam - in', for the los - er now will be
C/A
C/G
F
sink like a stone,
lat - er to win,
for the times, they are a -
C
F
1.
2.
chang - in'. Come

UNCHAINED MELODY

HORN

Lyric by HY ZARET
Music by ALEX NORTH

Moderately
G Em C D
Oh, my love, my dar - ling, I've hun - gered for your
Time goes by so slow - ly, and time can do so
G
touch a
much. Are
1.
Em D
long, lone - ly time.
2.
Em D G
you still mine? I need your love,
D Em Bm C
I need your love. God speed your love
D G
to me.
Fine
C
Lone - ly riv - ers
Lone - ly riv - ers
D C B♭ C
flow to the sea, to the sea, to the o - pen
sigh, "Wait for me, wait for me. I'll be com - ing
D
arms of the
home; wait for
1.
G
sea.
2.
G
me."
D.C. al Fine
(take repeat)

TOMORROW

from The Musical Production ANNIE

HORN

Lyric by MARTIN CHARNIN
Music by CHARLES STROUSE

Moderately fast

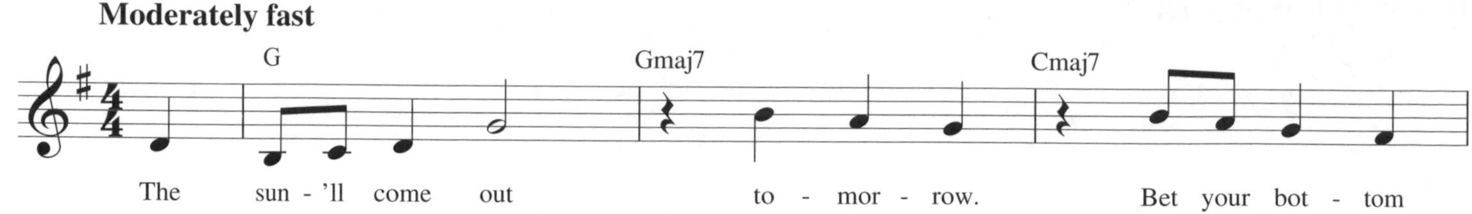
G
Gmaj7
Cmaj7
The sun - 'll come out to - mor - row. Bet your bot - tom

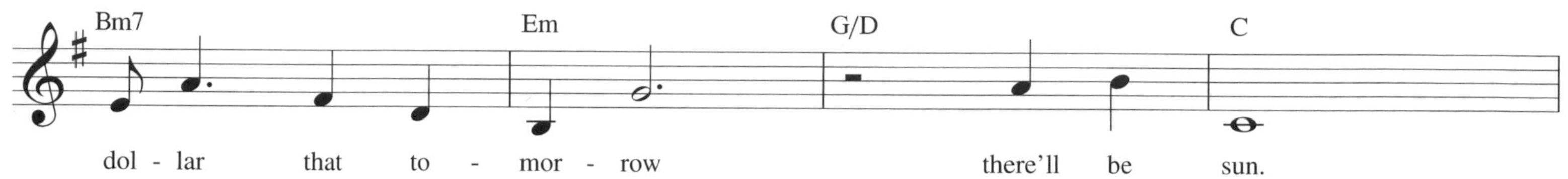
Bm7
Em
G/D
C
dol - lar that to - mor - row there'll be sun.

D
G
Gmaj7
Cmaj7
Just think - ing a - bout to - mor - row clears a - way the

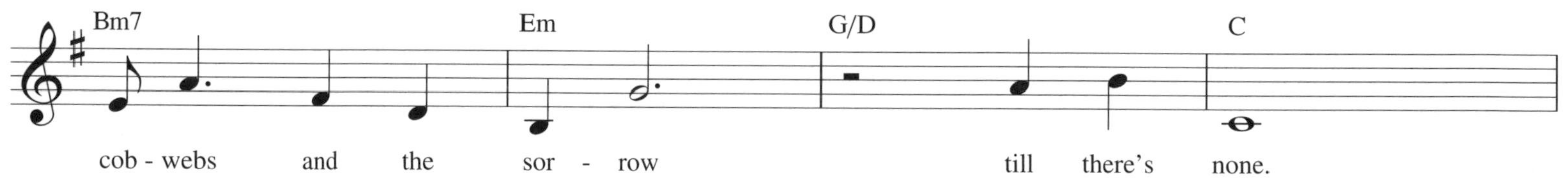
Bm7
Em
G/D
C
cob - webs and the sor - row till there's none.

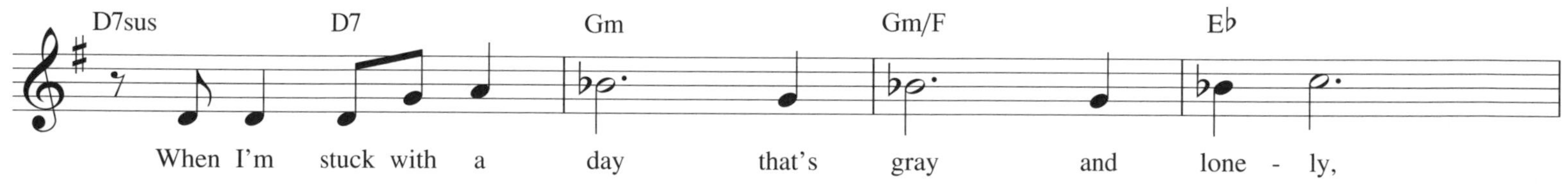
D7sus
D7
Gm
Gm/F
E♭
When I'm stuck with a day that's gray and lone - ly,

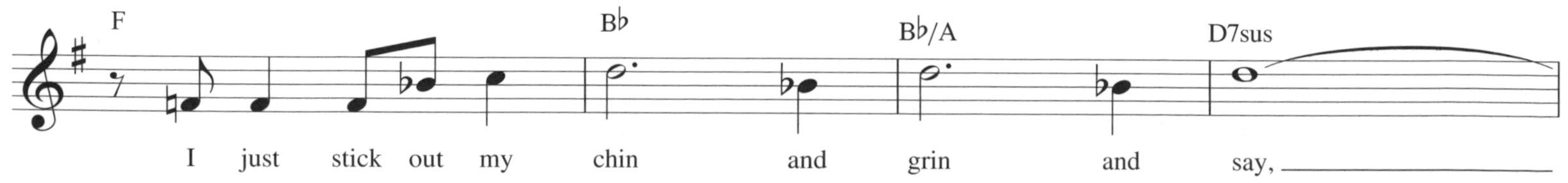
F
B♭
B♭/A
D7sus
I just stick out my chin and grin and say,

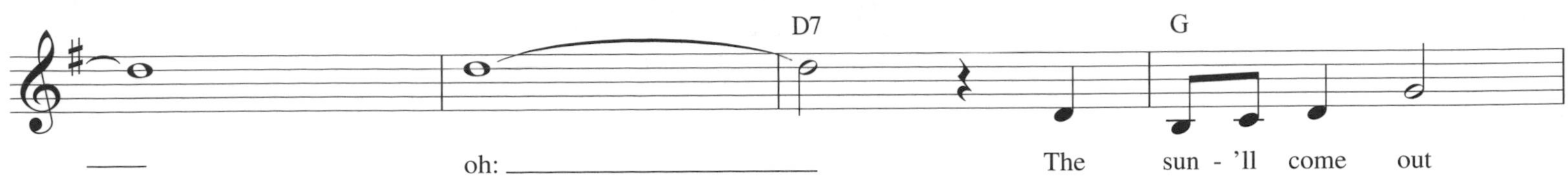
D7
G
oh:
The sun - 'll come out

Gmaj7
Cmaj7
Bm7
Em
to - mor - row, so you got - ta hang on till to - mor - row,

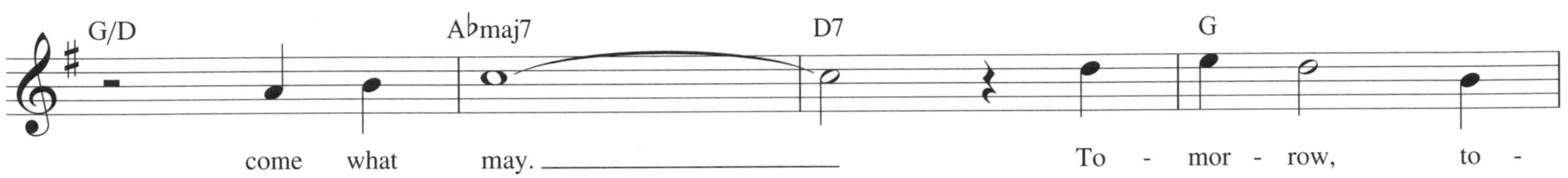
G/D
A♭maj7
D7
G
come what may. To - mor - row, to -

Gmaj7
G7
C
Cm
G/D
mor - row, I love ya, to - mor - row. You're al - ways a

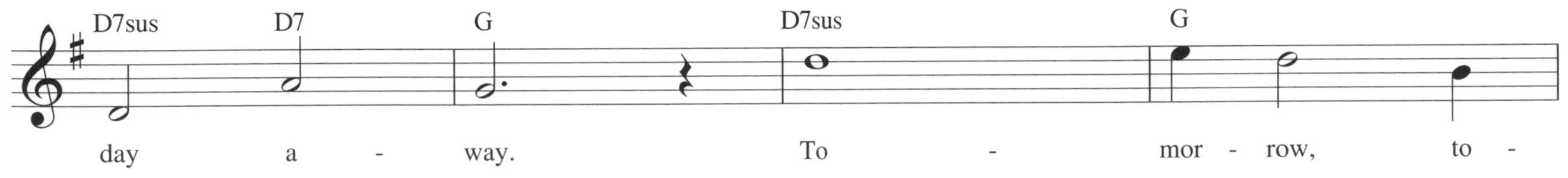
D7sus
D7
G
D7sus
G
day a - way. To - mor - row, to -

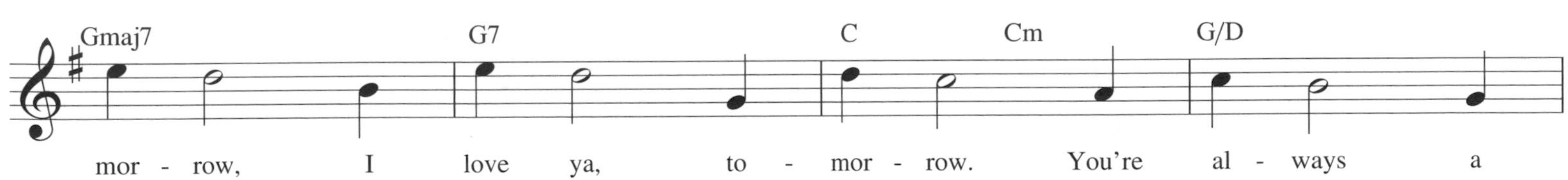
Gmaj7
G7
C
Cm
G/D
mor - row, I love ya, to - mor - row. You're al - ways a

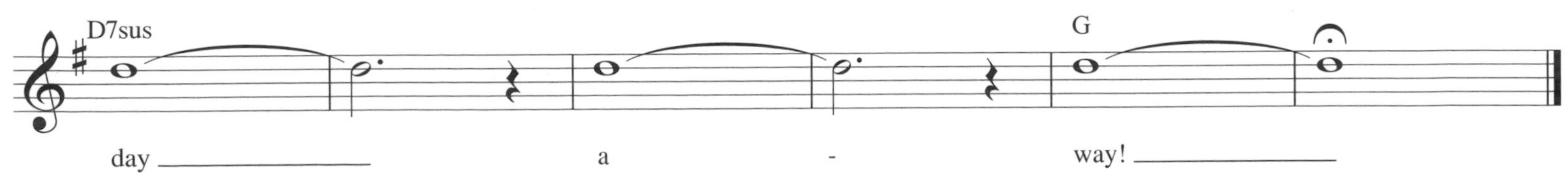
D7sus
G
day a - way!

VIVA LA VIDA

HORN

Words and Music by GUY BERRYMAN,
JON BUCKLAND, WILL CHAMPION
and CHRIS MARTIN

Moderately

B♭
C7sus
F
I used to rule the world. Seas would rise when I gave the word.

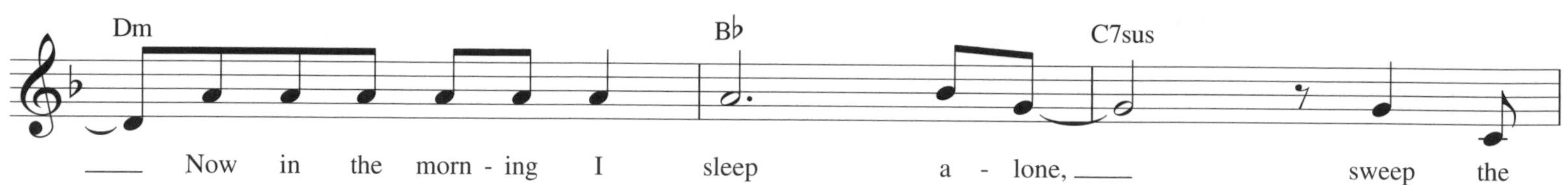
Dm
B♭
C7sus
Now in the morn - ing I sleep a - lone, sweep the

F
Dm
B♭
C7sus
streets I used to own.

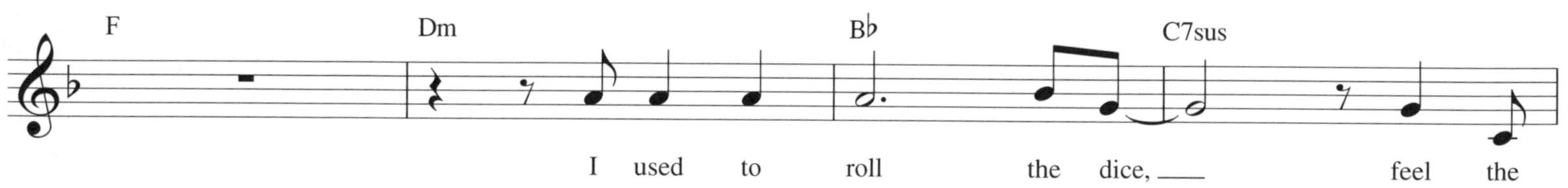
F
Dm
B♭
C7sus
I used to roll the dice, feel the

F
Dm
B♭
fear in my en - e - my's eyes, lis - ten as the crowd would sing,

C7sus
F
Dm
"Now the old king is dead; long live the king." One min - ute I

B♭
C7sus
F
held the key, next the walls were closed on

Dm
B♭
C7sus
me. And I dis - cov - ered that my cas - tles stand upon

F
Dm
B♭5
pil - lars of salt and pil - lars of sand. I hear Je - ru - sa - lem bells

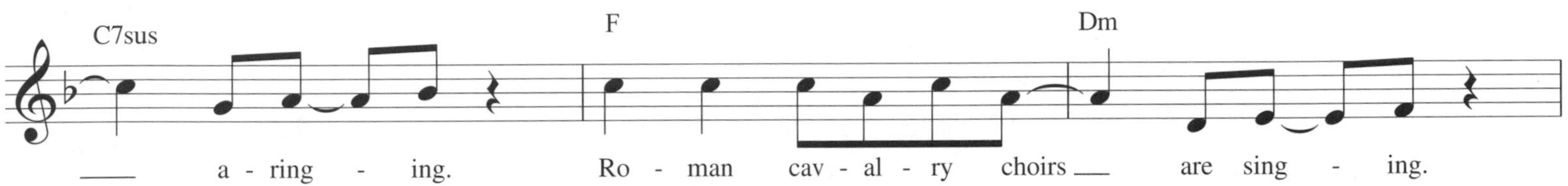
C7sus
F
Dm
a - ring - ing. Ro - man cav - al - ry choirs are sing - ing.

B♭5
C7sus
F
Be my mir - ror, my sword and shield, my mis - sion - ar - ies in a for -

Dm
B♭5
C7sus
- eign field. For some rea - son I can't ex - plain,

F
Dm
B♭5
once you've gone there was nev - er, nev - er an hon - est word,

C7sus
F
Dm
and that was when I ruled the world.

WE ARE THE WORLD

HORN

Words and Music by LIONEL RICHIE
and MICHAEL JACKSON

Moderately

F Bb/F C/F F

There comes a time __ when we heed a cer - tain call, __ when the
We can't go on __ pre - tend - ing day __ by day __ that some -

Bb C F

world must come to - geth - er as one. There are peo -
one some - where will soon make a change. We are all __

Dm Am7

- ple dy - ing, oh, and it's time ___ to lend a hand to life, __
__ a part __ of God's __ great ___ big fam - i - ly, and the

Gm7 Bb 1. Csus C 2. Csus

__ the great - est gift __ of all. ___
truth, you know love is all __ we need. ___

C Bb C F

__ We are the world, __ we are the chil - dren.

Bb C F

We are the ones __ who make a bright - er day, __ so let's __ start giv - ing.

Dm Am7

There's a choice we're mak - ing; ___ we're sav - ing our __ own lives. __

Gm7 C7sus F

__ It's true: __ we make a bet - ter day, __ just you __ and me. ___

WHAT A WONDERFUL WORLD

HORN

Words and Music by GEORGE DAVID WEISS
and BOB THIELE

Moderately slow
F Am B♭ Am Gm F
I see trees of green, red ros - es too. I see them bloom
skies of blue and clouds of white, the bright blessed day,
ba - bies cry; I watch them grow. They'll learn much more
To Coda
A7 Dm D♭ Gm7 C7
for me and you.
the dark sacred night. And I think to my - self: What a won - der - ful
than I'll ever know.
1. F B9♭5 B♭maj7 C7
world! I see
2. F Gm/F F
world! The
B♭/C C7 Fmaj7 F6 B♭/C C7
col - ors of the rain - bow, so pret - ty in the sky, are al - so on the fac - es of
Fmaj7 F6 Dm C/E Dm C
peo - ple go - ing by. I see friends shak - ing hands, say - ing, "How do you do?"
D.S. al Coda
Dm F♯dim7 Gm7 C7
They're real - ly say - ing, "I love you." I hear
CODA
F E♭7♭5 D9 D7♭9 D7
world! I
Gm7 C7♭9 F Gm/F F
think to my - self: What a won - der - ful world!

WONDERWALL

HORN
Words and Music by
NOEL GALLAGHER
Moderately fast
Dm7
F
Csus
G7sus
Bb(add9)
C
To - day is gon - na be the day that they're gon - na throw it back to you.
Back - beat, the word was on the street that the fi - re in your heart is out.
By now you should-'ve some - how re - al - ized what you got - ta do.
I'm sure you've heard it all be - fore, but you never real - ly had a doubt.
I don't be - lieve that an - y - bod - y feels the way I do a - bout you now.
1.
2.
And all the roads we have to walk are wind - ing, and all

B♭(add9)
C
Dm7
the lights that lead us there are blind - ing.

B♭(add9)
C
F
C/E
There are man - y things that I would like to say to you,

Dm7
F
G7sus
but I don't know how.

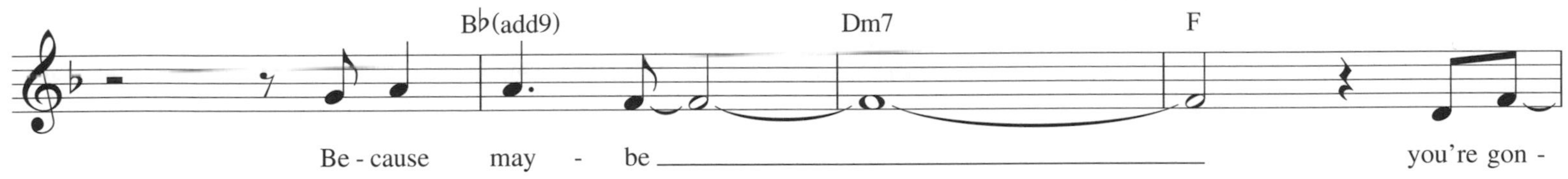
B♭(add9)
Dm7
F
Be - cause may - be you're gon -

Dm7
B♭(add9)
Dm7
F
- na be the one that saves me, and

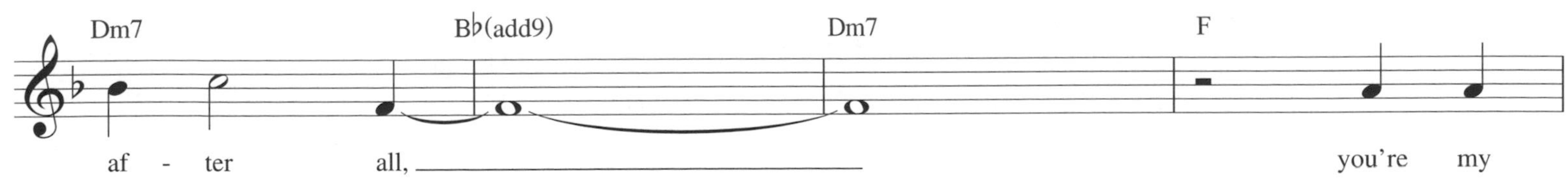
Dm7
B♭(add9)
Dm7
F
af - ter all, you're my

Dm7
B♭(add9)
Dm7
F
Dm7
won - der - wall.

YOU ARE THE SUNSHINE OF MY LIFE

HORN

Words and Music by
STEVIE WONDER

Brightly

F
C/B♭
Am7
D13♭9
You are the sun - shine of my life.
You are the ap - ple of my eye.

Gm7
B♭/C
F
Fine
Gm7
B♭/C
That's why I'll al - ways be a - round.
For - ev - er you'll stay in my heart.

Fmaj7
B♭
B♭/C
Fmaj7
B♭
B♭/C
I feel like this is the be - gin - ning,

Fmaj7
B♭
B♭/C
Em7♭5
A7
though I've loved you for a thou - sand years.

Dmaj7
G
G/A
Dm7
And if I thought our love was end - ing,
I'd find

G7
C7
D.C. al Fine
(take repeat)
my - self drown - ing in my own tears.
Whoa, whoa.

YOU'VE GOT A FRIEND

HORN

Words and Music by
CAROLE KING

Moderately
Am E7/B Am E7/B
When you're down and trou - bled and you need some lov - in' care
a - bove you grows dark and full of clouds
Am/C E7/B Am Dm7 G7 C
and noth - in', noth - in' is go - in' right,
and that old north wind be - gins to blow,
Bm7 E7 Am E7/B
close your eyes and think of me and soon I will be there
keep your head to - geth - er and call my name out loud.
Am/C E7/B Am Dm7 Em7 F/G G
to bright - en up e - ven your dark - est night.
Soon you'll hear me knock - in' at your door.
F/G C F
You just call out my name and you know wher - ev - er I am,
C F6/G
I'll come run - nin' to see you a - gain.
C Cmaj9 Fmaj7 F6 Am C7/G
Win - ter, spring, sum - mer or fall, all you have to do is call and I'll be
Fmaj7 Em7 Dm7 F/G C 1. Bm7 E7 2.
there, yes, I will. You've got a friend. If the sky

Audio Access Included

HAL•LEONARD EASY INSTRUMENTAL PLAY-ALONG

- Perfect for beginning players
- Carefully edited to include only the notes and rhythms that students learn in the first months playing their instrument
- Great-sounding demonstration and play-along tracks
- Audio tracks can be accessed online for download or streaming, using the unique code inside the book

HAL•LEONARD
EASY INSTRUMENTAL PLAY-ALONG
Audio Access Included
DISNEY FOR FLUTE
10 CLASSIC SONGS
INCLUDING: Can You Feel the Love Tonight • Mickey Mouse March
Part of Your World • Whistle While You Work • You'll Be in My Heart
Disney
HAL•LEONARD

HAL•LEONARD
EASY INSTRUMENTAL PLAY-ALONG
Audio Access Included
CLASSIC ROCK FOR FLUTE
10 MONUMENTAL HITS
INCLUDING: Another One Bites the Dust • Brown Eyed Girl
Fly Like an Eagle • I Heard It Through the Grapevine • Oye Como Va
HAL•LEONARD

HAL•LEONARD
EASY INSTRUMENTAL PLAY-ALONG
Audio Access Included
CLASSICAL THEMES FOR FLUTE
10 FAVORITE MELODIES
INCLUDING: Can Can • Carnival of Venice • Largo
Morning • Ode to Joy • Spring • Trumpet Voluntary
HAL•LEONARD

DISNEY

Book with Online Audio Tracks

The Ballad of Davy Crockett • Can You Feel the Love Tonight • Candle on the Water • I Just Can't Wait to Be King • The Medallion Calls • Mickey Mouse March • Part of Your World • Whistle While You Work • You Can Fly! You Can Fly! You Can Fly! • You'll Be in My Heart (Pop Version).

00122184 Flute $9.99
00122185 Clarinet $9.99
00122186 Alto Sax $9.99
00122187 Tenor Sax $9.99
00122188 Trumpet $9.99
00122189 Horn $9.99
00122190 Trombone $9.99
00122191 Violin $9.99
00122192 Viola $9.99
00122193 Cello $9.99
00122194 Keyboard Percussion $9.99

Disney characters and artwork © Disney Enterprises, Inc.

CLASSIC ROCK

Book with Online Audio Tracks

Another One Bites the Dust • Born to Be Wild • Brown Eyed Girl • Dust in the Wind • Every Breath You Take • Fly like an Eagle • I Heard It Through the Grapevine • I Shot the Sheriff • Oye Como Va • Up Around the Bend.

00122195 Flute $9.99
00122196 Clarinet $9.99
00122197 Alto Sax $9.99
00122198 Tenor Sax $9.99
00122201 Trumpet $9.99
00122202 Horn $9.99
00122203 Trombone $9.99
00122205 Violin $9.99
00122206 Viola $9.99
00122207 Cello $9.99
00122208 Keyboard Percussion $9.99

CLASSICAL THEMES

Book with Online Audio Tracks

Can Can • Carnival of Venice • Finlandia • Largo from Symphony No. 9 ("New World") • Morning • Musette in D Major • Ode to Joy • Spring • Symphony No. 1 in C Minor, Fourth Movement Excerpt • Trumpet Voluntary.

00123108 Flute $9.99
00123109 Clarinet $9.99
00123110 Alto Sax $9.99
00123111 Tenor Sax $9.99
00123112 Trumpet $9.99
00123113 Horn $9.99
00123114 Trombone $9.99
00123115 Violin $9.99
00123116 Viola $9.99
00123117 Cello $9.99
00123118 Keyboard Percussion $9.99

HAL•LEONARD®
CORPORATION

7777 W. Bluemound Rd. P.O. Box 13819 Milwaukee, WI 53213

www.halleonard.com

Prices, content, and availability subject to change without notice.

1113